14th Workshop on Building and Using Comparable Corpora (BUCC 2021)

In Conjunction with the 13th International Conference on Recent Advances in Natural Language Processing (RANLP 2021)

Online
6 September 2021

Editors:

Richard Rapp
Serge Sharoff
Pierre Zweigenbaum

ISBN: 978-1-7138-4098-5

Printed from e-media with permission by:

Curran Associates, Inc.
57 Morehouse Lane
Red Hook, NY 12571

Some format issues inherent in the e-media version may also appear in this print version.

Printed with permission by Curran Associates, Inc. (2022)

For permission requests, please contact the Association for Computational Linguistics at the address below.

Association for Computational Linguistics
209 N. Eighth Street
Stroudsburg, Pennsylvania 18360

Phone: 1-570-476-8006
Fax: 1-570-476-0860

acl@aclweb.org

Additional copies of this publication are available from:

Curran Associates, Inc.
57 Morehouse Lane
Red Hook, NY 12571 USA
Phone: 845-758-0400
Fax: 845-758-2633
Email: curran@proceedings.com
Web: www.proceedings.com

BUCC 2021

Proceedings
of the
14th Workshop on Building and Using Comparable Corpora (BUCC 2021)

in conjunction with

International Conference on Recent Advances in Natural Language Processing (RANLP 2021)

Edited by

Reinhard Rapp, Serge Sharoff, Pierre Zweigenbaum

September 6, 2021

14th Workshop on Building and Using Comparable Corpora (BUCC 2021)
in conjuction with
the International Conference Recent Advances in Natural Language Processing (RANLP 2021)

PROCEEDINGS

6 September 2021

Designed by INCOMA Ltd.
Shoumen, BULGARIA

14th BUCC Workshop at RANLP 2021 – Preface

Comparable corpora are collections of documents that are comparable in content and form in various degrees and dimensions. This definition includes many types of parallel and non-parallel multilingual corpora, but also sets of monolingual corpora that are used for comparative purposes. Research on comparable corpora is active but used to be scattered among many workshops and conferences. The workshop series on "Building and Using Comparable Corpora" (BUCC) aims at promoting progress in this exciting field by bundling some of its research, thereby making it more visible and giving it a better platform.

The first 12 editions of the workshop took place in Africa (LREC'08 in Marrakech), America (ACL'11 in Portland and ACL'17 in Vancouver), Asia (ACL-IJCNLP'09 in Singapore, ACL-IJCNLP'15 in Beijing, LREC'18 in Miyazaki, Japan), Europe (LREC'10 in Malta, ACL'13 in Sofia, LREC'14 in Reykjavik, LREC'16 in Portoroz, RANLP'19 in Varna) and also on the border between Asia and Europe (LREC'12 in Istanbul). Due to the corona crisis, the 13th edition took place online as an LREC'20 workshop. This year's 14th edition was held again online and took place as an RANLP'21 workshop.

We would like to thank all people who in one way or another helped in making this workshop once again a success. We are especially grateful to Ruslan Mitkov, Galia Angelova, Ivelina Nikolova, Kiril Simov and the whole RANLP team for their excellent support.

Our special thanks go to Pushpak Bhattacharyya, Tomas Mikolov and Sujith Ravi for accepting to give invited presentations and to the members of the programme committee who did an excellent job in reviewing the submitted papers under strict time constraints. Last but not least we would like to thank our authors, presenters and all participants of the workshop.

Reinhard Rapp, Serge Sharoff, Pierre Zweigenbaum — September 2021

Workshop Organizers:

Reinhard Rapp, Athena R.C., Magdeburg-Stendal University of Applied Sciences, University of Mainz (Chair)
Serge Sharoff, University of Leeds
Pierre Zweigenbaum, Université Paris-Saclay, CNRS, LISN

Programme Committee:

Ahmet Aker (University of Sheffield, UK)
Ebrahim Ansari (Institute for Advanced Studies in Basic Sciences, Iran)
Thierry Etchegoyhen (VicomTech, Spain)
Hitoshi Isahara (Otemon Gakuin University, Japan)
Kyo Kageura (The University of Tokyo, Japan)
Natalie Kübler (CLILLAC-ARP, Université de Paris, France
Philippe Langlais (Université de Montréal, Canada
Yves Lepage (Waseda University, Japan)
Emmanuel Morin (Université de Nantes, France)
Dragos Stefan Munteanu (Language Weaver, Inc., USA)
Reinhard Rapp (Athena R.C., Magdeburg-Stendal University of Applied Sciences, University of Mainz)
Nasredine Semmar (CEA LIST, Paris, France)
Serge Sharoff (University of Leeds, UK)
Richard Sproat (OGI School of Science & Technology, USA)
Tim Van de Cruys (KU Leuven, Belgium)
Pierre Zweigenbaum (Université Paris-Saclay, CNRS, LISN, Orsay, France)

Invited Speakers:

Pushpak Bhattacharyya, Indian Institute of Technology Bombai
Tomas Mikolov, Czech Institute of Informatics, Robotics and Cybernetics
Sujith Ravi, SliceX AI

Table of Contents

BUCC 2021 Workshop Programme

Monday, September 6, 2021

Times refer to UTC + 0

08:00–8:05 ***Opening***

Session 1: Invited Presentation

08:05–9:00 *Machine Translation in Low Resource Setting*
Pushpak Bhattacharyya, IIT Bombay

Session 2: Corpus Construction

9:00–9:25 *EM Corpus: a comparable corpus for a less-resourced language pair Manipuri-English*
Rudali Huidrom, Yves Lepage and Khogendra Khomdram

9:25–9:40 ***Coffee Break***

Session 3: Data Extraction and Corpus Annotation

9:40–10:05 *Mining Bilingual Word Pairs from Comparable Corpus using Apache Spark Framework*
Sanjanasri JP, Vijay Krishna Menon, Soman KP and Krzysztof Wolk

10:05–10:30 *Employing Wikipedia as a resource for Named Entity Recognition in Morphologically complex under-resourced languages*
Aravind Krishnan, Stefan Ziehe, Franziska Pannach and Caroline Sporleder

10:30–10:55 *Semi-Automated Labeling of Requirement Datasets for Relation Extraction*
Jeremias Bohn, Jannik Fischbach, Martin Schmitt, Hinrich Schütze and Andreas Vogelsang

10:55–11:20 *A Dutch Dataset for Cross-lingual Multilabel Toxicity Detection*
Ben Burtenshaw and Mike Kestemont

11:20–12:10 ***Lunch Break***

Session 4: Invited Presentation

12:10–13:05 *Language Modeling and AI*
Tomas Mikolov, Czech Institute of Informatics, Robotics and Cybernetics

Session 5: Neural MT and Bitext Extraction

13:05–13:30 *Syntax-aware Transformers for Neural Machine Translation: The Case of Text to Sign Gloss Translation*
Santiago Egea Gómez, Euan McGill and Horacio Saggion

13:30–13:55 *Effective Bitext Extraction From Comparable Corpora Using a Combination of Three Different Approaches*
Steinþór Steingrímsson, Pintu Lohar, Hrafn Loftsson and Andy Way

13:55–14:10 ***Coffee Break***

Session 6: Bitext Retrieval and Dictionary Extraction

14:10–14:35 *Majority Voting with Bidirectional Pre-translation For Bitext Retrieval*
Alexander Jones and Derry Tanti Wijaya

14:35–15:00 *On Pronunciations in Wiktionary: Extraction and Experiments on Multilingual Syllabification and Stress Prediction*
Winston Wu and David Yarowsky

Session 7: Invited Presentation

15:00–15:55 *Large-scale Deep Learning for Low-Resource AI*
Sujith Ravi, SliceX AI

15:55–16:00 ***Closing***

Invited Presentation

Machine Translation in Low Resource Setting

Pushpak Bhattacharyya
Computer Science and Engineering Department
Indian Institute of Technology Bombay

Abstract

AI now and in future will have to grapple continuously with the problem of low resource. AI will increasingly be ML intensive. But ML needs data often with annotation. However, annotation is costly.

Over the years, through work on multiple problems, we have developed insight into how to do language processing in low resource setting. Following 6 methods—individually and in combination—seem to be the way forward:

1. Artificially augment resource (e.g. subwords)

2. Cooperative NLP (e.g., pivot in MT)

3. Linguistic embellishment (e.g. factor based MT, source reordering)

4. Joint Modeling (e.g., Coref and NER, Sentiment and Emotion: each task helping the other to either boost accuracy or reduce resource requirement)

5. Multimodality (e.g., eye tracking based NLP, also picture+text+speech based Sentiment Analysis)

6. Cross Lingual Embedding (e.g., embedding from multiple languages helping MT, close to 2 above)

The present talk will focus on low resource machine translation. We describe the use of techniques from the above list and bring home the seriousness and methodology of doing Machine Translation in low resource settings.

Proceedings of 14th Workshop on Building and Using Comparable Corpora in conjunction with RANLP-2021, page 1, held online, 6 September 2021.
https://doi.org/10.26615/978-954-452-076-2_001

Mining Bilingual Word Pairs from Comparable Corpus using Apache Spark Framework

Sanjanasri JP[1], Vijay Krishna Menon[2], Soman KP[1], and Krzysztof Wolk[3]

[1]Center for Computational Engineering and Networking, Amrita School of Engineering, Coimbatore - 641112, India
[2]Gadgeon Systems Private Limited, Kochi, Kerala, India
[3] Department of Multimedia, Polish-Japanese Institute of Information Technology, Warsaw 02-008, Poland
jp_sanjanasri@cb.amrita.edu, vijay.km@gadgeon.com, kwolk@pja.edu.pl

Abstract

Bilingual dictionaries are essential resources in many areas of natural language processing tasks, but resource-scarce and less popular language pairs rarely have such. Efficient automatic methods for inducting bilingual dictionaries are needed as manual resources and efforts are scarce for low-resourced languages. In this paper, we induce word translations using bilingual embedding. We use the Apache Spark® framework for parallel computation. Further, to validate the quality of the generated bilingual dictionary, we use it in a phrase-table aided Neural Machine Translation (NMT) system. The system can perform moderately well with a manual bilingual dictionary; we change this into our inducted dictionary. The corresponding translated outputs are compared using the Bilingual Evaluation Understudy (BLEU) and Rank-based Intuitive Bilingual Evaluation Score (RIBES) metrics.

1 Introduction

Digitised bilingual dictionaries primarily exist for resource-rich language pairs, such as English-German, English- Chinese, English-Hindi, etc. (Lardilleux et al., 2010). Such dictionaries are helpful for many natural language processing (NLP) tasks such as Machine Translation (MT) for translating Out-Of-Vocabulary (OOV) words, cross-lingual information retrieval, cross-lingual word embedding and multilingual parts-of-speech tagging (Wołk, 2019; Ye et al., 2016; Sharma and Mittal, 2018). Creating a bilingual dictionary requires high-quality parallel corpora and expert linguists, both of which are scarce and costly in resource-poor languages (Hajnicz et al., 2016; Sarma, 2019).

Previous works focus on methods that were based on pivot languages (Tanaka and Umemura, 1994; István and Shoichi, 2009; Wushouer et al., 2015), aligning words (Daille and Morin, 2008; Tufiş and maria Barbu, 2002) or using dependency relations (Yu and Tsujii, 2009). The pivot-based dictionary induction is a contemporary method that uses only dictionaries to and from a pivot language (intermediate language) to generate a new dictionary. This method is not very effective for highly ambiguous languages as it yields highly noisy dictionaries because lexicons of a language do not exhibit transitive relationship (Wushouer et al., 2014). Word alignment systems identify the translation equivalence of lexical units between two sentences that are sentence aligned (Choueka et al., 2000; Och and Ney, 2003). Depending on the purpose, the system may focus on the specific lexical units, e.g. a single word or collocation (Tiedemann, 2004; Schreiner et al., 2011; Chen et al., 2009). The dependency relation method is based on the premise that related words in different languages have a similar dependency relationship. These methods require either excellent linguistic knowledge or linguistic resource. The research line has robust outcomes on bilingual lexicon induction with the evolution of word embedding either by independently aligning trained word embedding in two languages or using the bilingual embedding to induce word translation pairs through nearest-neighbour or similar retrieval methods. In the BDI task, given a list of 'n' source language words $w_{s1}, w_{s2}, ...w_{s_n}$, the goal is to determine the most appropriate translationw_{t_i}, for each query word w_{s_i}. Finding a target language word embedding wv_{t_i} is accomplished by computing the nearest neighbour to the source word embedding wv_{s_i} in the shared semantic space, where cosine similarity is a measure between the embedding (Artetxe et al., 2019). However, this creates a phenomenon called hubness. In high-dimensional spaces, some data points, called hubs, are extraordinarily close to many other data points (Huang et al., 2019); this results in inappropriate/noisy translation.

In this paper, a simple cartesian product of the bilingual/cross-lingual word embedding is used

Proceedings of 14th Workshop on Building and Using Comparable Corpora in conjunction with RANLP-2021, pages 2–7, held online, 6 September 2021.
https://doi.org/10.26615/978-954-452-076-2_002

and filters the product outcome based on some linguistic regularities and thresholds. The generated (inducted) bilingual dictionary is used as a separate phrase-table in an NMT system. The system produces translations for every word in the text; the translations are validated for quality using the Bilingual Evaluation Understudy (BLEU) and Rank-based Intuitive Bilingual Evaluation Score (RIBES) metric.

2 Bilingual and Cross-lingual Word embedding

In this paper, the terms 'bilingual' and 'cross-lingual' for word embedding is used with varying notions. The bilingual embedding maps the source and target language embedding in the shared semantic space. In contrast, the cross-lingual embedding learns a transfer function to translate the embedding from the source language semantic space to target language space; this preserves the more actual semantics pertained to that language (Mikolov et al., 2013). Visualisation of the embeddings is shown in Figure 1 and Figure 2.

BilBOWA toolkit (Gouws et al., 2015) is used to generate bilingual word embedding. The embedding of source and target language are trained jointly so that related words of two languages are closer to each other in the shared space. Therefore, the translational equivalence has higher cosine similarity. The model is trained with minimal parallel corpus and large monolingual corpora. However, the cross-lingual embedding is learned with a very bare minimal resource as small as 5000 source-target word pairs. Global neighbourhood is estimated as cross-lingual entropy. The main advantage of this method over bilingual embedding is that it is possible to generate embedding in the target language semantic space instead of shared space. In shared semantic space, the most semantic information pertained to the language is lost and likely to infer word vectors for related languages.

3 Implementation

The embedding size of the English word list is $\in \mathbb{R}^{8994\times300}$ and Tamil is $\in \mathbb{R}^{10097\times300}$. Tamil has more number words compared to English because of the inflected forms. The dimension of the Cartesian product of the word pair list (English and Tamil) is 90812418×300; this takes months for a typical computer system to compute. This complex computation is deployed to the cluster

Figure 1: Visualization of Bilingual Embedding using T-SNE plot

using Apache Spark® Framework (Zaharia et al., 2016). The word pairs are filtered in two folds, cosine similarity and lemmatization (Kengatharaiyer et al., 2019), where the root word is extracted from the surface forms. In the case of cross-lingual embedding, cross-lingual entropy is used instead of the cosine similarity measure. Figure 3 shows the architecture.

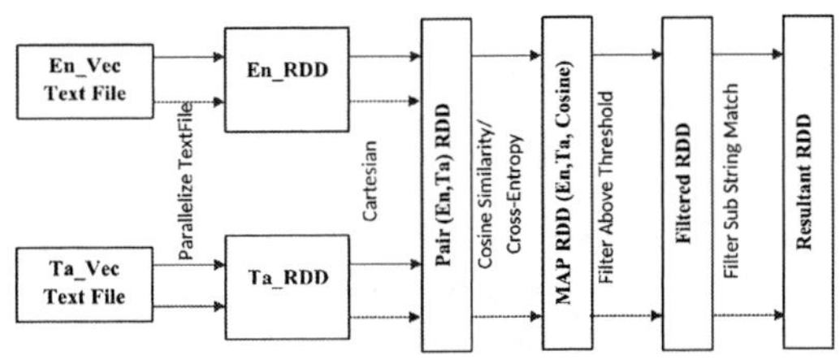

Figure 3: Apache Spark Implementation for Bilingual Dictionary Induction

The word embedding of Source and Target Language is mapped to a key-value pair Resilient Distributed Datasets (RDDs), a fundamental data structure of Spark; the word being a key and 300-dimensional representation as values. The Cartesian Product of two RDDs (En_RDD and Ta_RDD) generates the Pair RDD. On the Pair RDD, cosine similarity or cross-lingual entropy is applied to filter top similar words. Filtered RDD is further refined using a lemmatizer to avoid the inflected terms. The resultant RDD is saved as text file; this has the most similar source and target word, a bilingual dictionary.

The OpenNMT framework (Klein et al., 2017) is used for training an NMT system with the training parameter as shown in Table 1. The inducted lexi-

(a) English Embedding Space

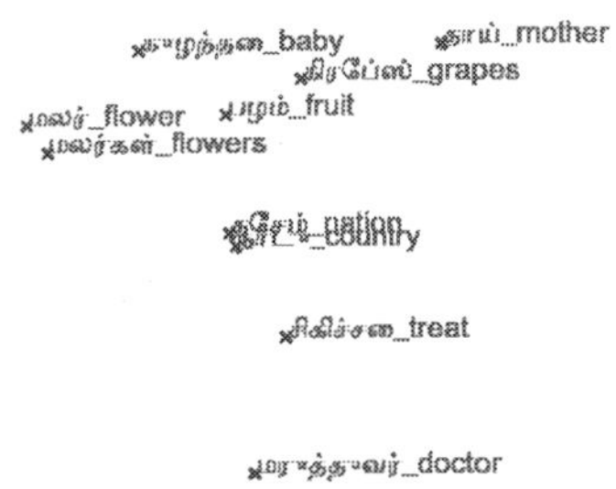

(b) Tamil Embedding Space

Figure 2: Visualization of Cross-lingual embedding using T-SNE plot

cons are used as a phrase-table in NMT for translating Out-Of-Vocabulary (OOV) words. Training is done on Google Colab with GPU at backend.

Table 1: Training Parameters for English-Tamil OpenNMT Framework

Hyper Parameters	Values
Layers	3
Rnn_size	512
Embedding_size	512
Encoder/Decoder Type	Transformers
Train_steps / Validation_steps	3000/ 5000
Positional Encoding	True
Heads	8
Dropout	0.3
Learning rate	3
Batch size	4096
Optimiser	ADAM

4 Corpora Description

For the training language model, the monolingual Tamil corpus from the cEnTam dataset (P. et al., 2020) is used. Likewise, for training the machine translation systems, the English-Tamil parallel corpus from the cEnTam dataset is utilised. The specifics of the cEnTam corpus used is reported in Table 2.

Table 2: Specification of cEnTam Corpus

Corpus Type	English *(No. of sentences)*	Tamil *(No. of sentences)*
Monolingual	589856	563568
Parallel	56495	56495

5 Results and Discussion

Table 3 and 4 show a sample of bilingually similar words above the cosine distance of 0.90 and 0.95. The correct translations are given in bold letters in Table 3 and 4. It can be inferred that the much more words that are not semantically similar (translational equivalent) but related crowds the search space, which might result in noisy word inductions (into the dictionary) and ambiguity. Hence the search space was shrunk above the cosine distance of 0.98 as shown in Table 5. It is observed that the inflected forms (surface forms) are closer than the related words in the embedding space to the query word. Unlike English, Tamil has no prepositions. Instead, it has case inflected nouns, for example, the translation of the prepositional phrase "in minutes" in English is equivalent to "*NimidanGkaLil*", a case inflected noun(*NimidanGkaL + il* = minutes + in) in Tamil. Likewise, various sandhi inflected form of the noun "*kuzhanthai*" are *kuzhanthaip*, *kuzhanthaith*, etc. The chances of getting associated or related words in such a small space is negligible. The inflections are removed, and the root forms are inducted at the second stage of filtering, lemmatizer. The inducted dictionary is added as a lookup table in the NMT system.

Table 3: Sample output of bilingual words extracted above cosine similarity (threshold) 0.90

English	Tamil	Cosine Similarity
go	avaL	0.92
go	ennai	0.90
go	evvaLavu	0.90
go	anGkae	0.92
go	poaka	0.92
go	enGkae	0.90
go	un	0.90
good	**chariyaana**	**0.92**
good	aen	0.91
good	avaL	0.90
good	**nanRaaka**	**0.94**
good	evvaLavu	0.91

Table 4: Sample output of bilingual words extracted above cosine similarity 0.95

English	Tamil	Cosine Similarity
forests	pachumaiyaana	0.92
forests	adarNtha	0.95
forests	**kaadukaL**	**0.98**
flowers	malar	0.95
flowers	**malarkaL**	**0.97**
flowers	pookkaL	0.96

Table 5: Sample output of bilingual words extracted above cosine similarity 0.98. The exact translation of the query word is annotated with double raised asterisk ** and their inflected forms are annotated with single raised asterisk*.

English	Tamil	Cosine Similarity
minutes	NimidanGkaL **	0.98
minutes	NimidanGkaLil*	0.99
minutes	Nimidaththil *	0.97
minutes	NimidanGkaLaaka*	0.98

The accuracy of the translated sentence of the NMT system before and after appending the dictionary as a phrase table is shown in Table 6. The induced translation is evaluated based on both the Bilingual Evaluation Understudy (BLEU) (Koehn, 2010) and Rank-based Intuitive Bilingual Evaluation Score (RIBES) (Isozaki et al., 2010) metrics. BLEU is the oldest and most adopted metrics to evaluate Mt system. It rewards systems for n-grams that have exact matches in the reference system. The longer n-gram scores account for the fluency of the translation in BLEU metric. In contrast, RIBES is sensitive towards word reordering, works well for language pairs having very different grammar and word order. It uses rank correlation coefficients based on word order to compare hypothesis and reference translations.

Table 6: Precision of NMT system

NMT System	BLEU	RIBES
Reference-Baseline	0.31	0.61
Reference-ManDic	0.33	0.66
Reference-InDic	0.34	0.71
ManDic-InDic	0.89	0.95

Although BLEU is a standard metric for the evaluation of MT system, RIBES is better suited for distant language pairs like English and Tamil (Callison-Burch et al., 2006). Hence, both measures are used for validating the NMT system developed. In the Table 6, the score is computed by comparing the reference translations with the translations of the NMT system after appending the manual and inducted dictionary (ManDic & IndDic). The ManDic and InDic systems are compared to showcase that the hypothesis translation of InDic is highly correlated with ManDic, though InDic has comparatively better score than ManDic when validated against Reference translation.

6 Conclusion and Summary

In this paper, we generated an English-Tamil bilingual dictionary using both bilingual (vectors in the same space) and cross-lingual (vectors in separate space, mapped) word embedding. In order to validate this induced dictionary, we have employed a table driven Neural Machine Translation (NMT) system. The goal was to measure the quality of the translated output (Tamil as the target language) when the original manual dictionary (ManDic) is replaced with the induced dictionary (InDic). The Baseline NMT system was trained on English-Tamil parallel corpus with over 56000 entries. A testset with 700 aligned sentences was used for validation. The translation quality is measured over the reference translations which are available (aligned Tamil sentences). Eventually, we will have three categories of translated output, namely, Baseline, ManDic and InDic. We compare each of them with the reference translation using the RIBES and BLEU metric (Isozaki et al., 2010; Koehn, 2010) to ascertain their quality. It is important to note that the quality of the translations is not of our interest but the change in performance when using different dictionaries. RIBES is used as the scoring model as it is invariant to word order and morphology (Tan et al., 2015).

Our results suggest that the induced dictionary performs at par or better than the original manual dictionary. This is also due to the fact that the lexicons are rendered in a context-sensitive manner from word embedding. The lookup process is implemented using Apache Spark® Framework in Scala language. Induction is a simple reverse lookup using the Cartesian product of all bilingual embedding. The size of this Cartesian product matrix is $1 \times 10^7 \times 300$ values which makes it highly computational. Apache Spark can run in parallel, hence, accelerate time and optimise memory. In this paper, bilingual embedding generated by BilBOWA (Gouws et al., 2015) is mainly used, but this methodology is also tested with cross-lingual embedding and found equally effective (JP et al.,

2020). The differences between them are: bilingual embeddings are generated from parallel and good quality comparable bilingual corpus, whereas cross-lingual embedding can be learned from minimal bilingual data. Learning such cross-lingual embedding for resource-poor languages can help to generate induced dictionary resources of even unknown words with a fair amount of accuracy.

References

Mikel Artetxe, Gorka Labaka, and Eneko Agirre. 2019. Bilingual lexicon induction through unsupervised machine translation. In *Proceedings of the 57th Annual Meeting of the Association for Computational Linguistics*, pages 5002–5007, Florence, Italy. Association for Computational Linguistics.

Chris Callison-Burch, Miles Osborne, and Philipp Koehn. 2006. Re-evaluating the role of bleu in machine translation research. In *In EACL*, pages 249–256.

Yidong Chen, Xiaodong Shi, Changle Zhou, and Qingyang Hong. 2009. A word alignment model based on multiobjective evolutionary algorithms. *Computers & Mathematics with Applications*, 57(11):1724 – 1729. Proceedings of the International Conference.

Yaacov Choueka, Ehud S. Conley, and Ido Dagan. 2000. *A comprehensive bilingual word alignment system*, pages 69–96. Springer Netherlands, Dordrecht.

Béatrice Daille and Emmanuel Morin. 2008. An effective compositional model for lexical alignment. In *Proceedings of the Third International Joint Conference on Natural Language Processing: Volume-I.*

Stephan Gouws, Yoshua Bengio, and Greg Corrado. 2015. Bilbowa: Fast bilingual distributed representations without word alignments. In *ICML*, volume 37 of *JMLR Workshop and Conference Proceedings*, pages 748–756.

Elżbieta Hajnicz, Anna Andrzejczuk, and Tomasz Bartosiak. 2016. Semantic layer of the valence dictionary of Polish walenty. In *Proceedings of the Tenth International Conference on Language Resources and Evaluation (LREC'16)*, pages 2625–2632, Portorož, Slovenia. European Language Resources Association (ELRA).

Jiaji Huang, Qiang Qiu, and Kenneth Church. 2019. Hubless nearest neighbor search for bilingual lexicon induction. In *Proceedings of the 57th Annual Meeting of the Association for Computational Linguistics*, pages 4072–4080, Florence, Italy. Association for Computational Linguistics.

Hideki Isozaki, Tsutomu Hirao, Kevin Duh, Katsuhito Sudoh, and Hajime Tsukada. 2010. Automatic evaluation of translation quality for distant language pairs. In *Proceedings of the 2010 Conference on Empirical Methods in Natural Language Processing*, pages 944–952, Cambridge, MA. Association for Computational Linguistics.

Varga István and Yokoyama Shoichi. 2009. Bilingual dictionary generation for low-resourced language pairs. In *Proceedings of the 2009 Conference on Empirical Methods in Natural Language Processing: Volume 2 - Volume 2*, EMNLP '09, pages 862–870, Stroudsburg, PA, USA. Association for Computational Linguistics.

Sanjanasri JP, Vijay Krishna Menon, and Soman KP. 2020. BUCC2020: Bilingual dictionary induction using cross-lingual embedding. In *Proceedings of the 13th Workshop on Building and Using Comparable Corpora*, pages 65–68, Marseille, France. European Language Resources Association.

Sarveswaran Kengatharaiyer, Gihan Dias, and Miriam Butt. 2019. Thamizhifst: A morphological analyser and generator for tamil verbs.

Guillaume Klein, Yoon Kim, Yuntian Deng, Jean Senellart, and Alexander Rush. 2017. OpenNMT: Open-source toolkit for neural machine translation. In *Proceedings of ACL 2017, System Demonstrations*, pages 67–72, Vancouver, Canada. Association for Computational Linguistics.

Philipp Koehn. 2010. *Statistical Machine Translation*, 1st edition. Cambridge University Press, New York, NY, USA.

Adrien Lardilleux, Julien Gosme, and Yves Lepage. 2010. Bilingual lexicon induction: Effortless evaluation of word alignment tools and production of resources for improbable language pairs. In *Proceedings of the Seventh conference on International Language Resources and Evaluation (LREC'10)*, Valletta, Malta. European Languages Resources Association (ELRA).

Tomas Mikolov, Kai Chen, Greg Corrado, and Jeffrey Dean. 2013. Efficient estimation of word representations in vector space. *CoRR*, abs/1301.3781.

Franz Josef Och and Hermann Ney. 2003. A systematic comparison of various statistical alignment models. *Computational Linguistics*, 29(1):19–51.

Sanjanasri J. P., B. Premjith, Vijay Krishna Menon, and K. P. Soman. 2020. centam: Creation and validation of a new english-tamil bilingual corpus. In *Proceedings of the 13th Workshop on Building and Using Comparable Corpora, BUCC@LREC 2020, Marseille, France, May, 2020*, pages 61–64. European Language Resources Association.

Prof. Shikhar Kr. Sarma. 2019. Assamese-english bilingual dictionary. CLARIN-PL digital repository.

Paulo Schreiner, Aline Villavicencio, Leonardo Zilio, and Helena M. Caseli. 2011. Improving lexical alignment using hybrid discriminative and post-processing techniques. In *Proceedings of the 8th Brazilian Symposium in Information and Human Language Technology*.

Vijay Sharma and Namita Mittal. 2018. *Cross-Lingual Information Retrieval: A Dictionary-Based Query Translation Approach*, pages 611–618.

Li Ling Tan, Jonathan Dehdari, and Josef van Genabith. 2015. An awkward disparity between bleu / ribes scores and human judgements in machine translation. In *Proceedings of the Workshop on Asian Translation (WAT-2015)*, pages 74–81. Association for Computational Linguistics.

Kumiko Tanaka and Kyoji Umemura. 1994. Construction of a bilingual dictionary intermediated by a third language. In *Proceedings of the 15th Conference on Computational Linguistics - Volume 1*, COLING '94, pages 297–303, Stroudsburg, PA, USA. Association for Computational Linguistics.

Jörg Tiedemann. 2004. Word to word alignment strategies. In *Proceedings of the 20th International Conference on Computational Linguistics*, COLING '04, Stroudsburg, PA, USA. Association for Computational Linguistics.

Dan Tufiş and Ana maria Barbu. 2002. Lexical token alignment: experiments, results and applications. In *In Third International Conference on Language Resources and Evaluation (LREC 2002), Las Palmas*, pages 458–465.

Krzysztof Wołk. 2019. *Machine Learning in Translation Corpora Processing*.

Mairidan Wushouer, Donghui Lin, Toru Ishida, and Katsutoshi Hirayama. 2014. Pivot-based bilingual dictionary extraction from multiple dictionary resources. In *PRICAI 2014: Trends in Artificial Intelligence*, pages 221–234, Cham. Springer International Publishing.

Mairidan Wushouer, Donghui Lin, Toru Ishida, and Katsutoshi Hirayama. 2015. A constraint approach to pivot-based bilingual dictionary induction. *ACM Trans. Asian Low-Resour. Lang. Inf. Process.*, 15(1):4:1–4:26.

Zhonglin Ye, Zhen Jia, Junfu Huang, and Hongfeng Yin. 2016. Part-of-speech tagging based on dictionary and statistical machine learning. In *2016 35th Chinese Control Conference (CCC)*, pages 6993–6998.

Kun Yu and Junichi Tsujii. 2009. Extracting bilingual dictionary from comparable corpora with dependency heterogeneity. In *Proceedings of Human Language Technologies: The 2009 Annual Conference of the North American Chapter of the Association for Computational Linguistics, Companion Volume: Short Papers*, pages 121–124, Boulder, Colorado. Association for Computational Linguistics.

Matei Zaharia, Reynold S. Xin, Patrick Wendell, Tathagata Das, Michael Armbrust, Ankur Dave, Xiangrui Meng, Josh Rosen, Shivaram Venkataraman, Michael J. Franklin, Ali Ghodsi, Joseph Gonzalez, Scott Shenker, and Ion Stoica. 2016. Apache spark: A unified engine for big data processing. *Commun. ACM*, 59(11):56–65.

Effective Bitext Extraction From Comparable Corpora Using a Combination of Three Different Approaches

Steinþór Steingrímsson[1], Pintu Lohar[2], Hrafn Loftsson[1], and Andy Way[2]
[1]Department of Computer Science, Reykjavik University, Iceland;
[1]ADAPT Centre, School of Computing, Dublin City University, Ireland
steinthor18@ru.is, pintu.lohar@adaptcentre.ie,
hrafn@ru.is, andy.way@adaptcentre.ie

Abstract

Parallel sentences extracted from comparable corpora can be useful to supplement parallel corpora when training machine translation (MT) systems. This is even more prominent in low-resource scenarios, where parallel corpora are scarce. In this paper, we present a system which uses three very different measures to identify and score parallel sentences from comparable corpora. We measure the accuracy of our methods in low-resource settings by comparing the results against manually curated test data for English–Icelandic, and by evaluating an MT system trained on the concatenation of the parallel data extracted by our approach and an existing data set. We show that the system is capable of extracting useful parallel sentences with high accuracy, and that the extracted pairs substantially increase translation quality of an MT system trained on the data, as measured by automatic evaluation metrics.

1 Introduction

High quality MT systems rely on the availability of parallel data. In low-resource settings, where parallel data is scarce, unsupervised methods have been proposed, where only monolingual corpora are used for training (Artetxe et al., 2018; Lample et al., 2018). Kim et al. (2020) show that supervised and semi-supervised approaches with only a small parallel corpus of 50K bilingual sentences consistently outperform the best unsupervised systems for a range of languages. However, there is a scarcity of parallel data, especially for languages with a low number of speakers. When parallel corpora are scarce, comparable corpora, which are far more common, can be used to supplement it. We will be working with the English–Icelandic language pair, for which no statistical or neural MT work had been published until last year (Jónsson et al., 2020).

When parallel sentences are extracted from comparable corpora, potential parallel sentence candidates can usually come from anywhere in two comparable documents. This means that a potential parallel counterpart of one sentence in the source-language document can be any sentence in the target-language document. If the average number of sentences in a comparable document is n, the number of potential sentence pairs that have to be evaluated are n^2. This quickly becomes overwhelming (as n increases) and so it is imperative to reduce the search space. Reducing the search space should ideally result in a list of a maximum of kxn candidates, where k is a constant number of allowed candidates for each sentence in the comparable documents. To retrieve useful sentence pairs from this list, the pairs have to be scored and filtered.

Our approach divides the problem into two main steps. We start by extracting parallel sentence candidates using an inverted index-based crosslingual information retrieval (CLIR) tool called *FaDA* (Lohar et al., 2016), that requires a collection of documents in two languages and only a bilingual lexicon without the need of any MT system. In the second step, we score the sentence candidates using two different scores, one based on contextualized embeddings and the other on high-precision word alignments. A binary classifier selects sentence pairs based on these scores.

We test our approach in three different ways. We use two different test sets to measure precision, recall and F1-scores, and we also use our approach to extract parallel sentences from Wikipedia and use the resulting data as supplemental data for training NMT systems. The systems are then evaluated in terms of BLEU scores (Papineni et al., 2002) and compared to a baseline in order to give an indication of the usefulness of the supplemental data for NMT training.

Proceedings of 14th Workshop on Building and Using Comparable Corpora in conjunction with RANLP-2021, pages 8–17, held online, 6 September 2021.
https://doi.org/10.26615/978-954-452-076-2_003

Our main contributions are fourfold.

- We show that the combination of three different measures – CLIR, and scores based on contextualized embeddings and high precision word alignments – can effectively extract parallel sentence pairs from comparable corpora.
- We introduce WAScore, a score based on high precision word alignments and show its usefulness in filtering parallel sentence pairs.
- We publish two different test sets for measuring the effectiveness of parallel sentence extraction from comparable corpora for the English–Icelandic language pair.
- We publish a set of parallel sentences extracted from Wikipedia, shown to be useful for MT training.

2 Related Work

Comparable corpora have been shown to be a useful source for mining parallel segments that can help improve MT quality (Wolk et al., 2016; Hangya and Fraser, 2019). Afli et al. (2015) extract parallel data from a multimodal comparable corpus from the Euronews[1] and TED[2] web sites. Chu et al. (2015) extract parallel texts from the Chinese and Japanese Wikipedia and Ling et al. (2014) employ a crowdsourcing approach to extract parallel text from Twitter data in order to find the translations in tweets. The work of Karimi et al. (2018) describes the approach of extracting parallel sentences from English–Persian document-aligned Wikipedia entries. They use two MT systems to translate from Persian to English and the reverse and then use an IR system to measure the similarity of the translated sentences. Multilingual sentence embeddings have also been applied to the problem, obtaining state-of-the-art performance (Schwenk, 2018; Artetxe and Schwenk, 2019b). Recently, Ramesh et al. (2021) describe the collection of parallel corpora for 11 Indic languages from diverse comparable corpora using LaBSE embeddings (Feng et al., 2020), a language-agnostic BERT sentence embedding model trained and optimized to produce similar representations for bilingual sentence pairs that are translations of each other.

[1]https://www.euronews.com/

[2]https://www.ted.com/

Word alignments have previously been used for parallel sentence extraction. Zariņa et al. (2015) identify parallel sentences using word alignments, experimenting with five different alignment based scores. They presume that if a pair of sentences are equivalent in two languages, there should be many word alignments between the sentences, and non-parallel sentences should have few or no word alignments. Stymne et al. (2013) use alignment based heuristics to filter out sentence pairs. Lu et al. (2020) use a word alignment based translation score as a part of their scoring ensemble for filtering a noisy parallel corpus. Their translation score is a simplified version of the translation score introduced by Khadivi and Ney (2005). Azpeitia et al. (2017) and Andoni Azpeitia and Garcia (2018) describe a method using CLIR and lexical translations obtained using word alignments, with a simple overlap metric. They obtained the highest results for the BUCC 2017 and BUCC 2018 shared tasks.

Our method uses an IR system to create a list of alignment candidates, thus reducing the search space. It then takes advantage of both LaBSE embeddings and word alignments. Our word alignment score is calculated by a simpler formula than most of the previous work, but relies on high precision alignments. It has been shown that they can be achieved by an ensemble method using *CombAlign* (Steingrímsson et al., 2021). A binary classifier is finally used to select acceptable sentence pairs.

3 Data

For the language pair we are working with, English–Icelandic, no test sets have previously been made available for parallel sentence extraction from comparable corpora. Therefore, we have to build test sets in order to be able to evaluate our approach. We prepare the following data sets for our experiments:

- *CompNews*: development and test sets using available news data,
- *CompWiki*: a manually curated small test set for Wikipedia data,
- *CompTrain*: training data for our logistic regression classifier, and
- *CompLex*: an English–Icelandic lexicon for word translation in an IR system.

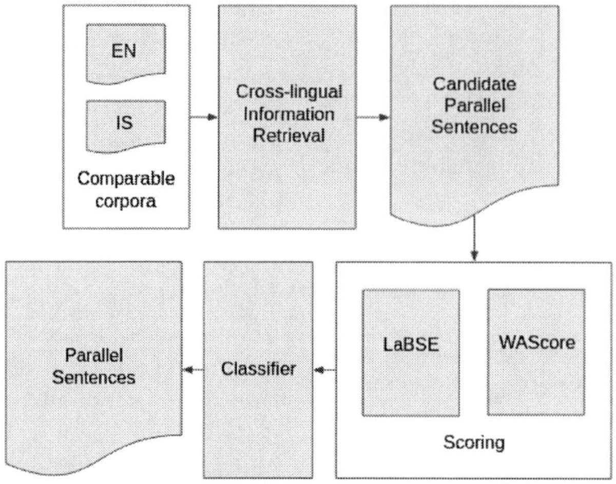

Figure 1: The system setup. English and Icelandic monolingual data are aligned by the CLIR system which outputs candidate pairs which are scored and a classifier outputs parallel sentence pairs.

All the data sets are published with open licenses on GitHub and in a CLARIN repository.

3.1 CompNews

We built development and test sets for identifying parallel sentences in news corpora, in similar style to the test sets compiled for the BUCC 2017 shared task on parallel sentence identification (Zweigenbaum et al., 2016), i.e. consisting of a small set of known parallel sentences, as well as a larger list of randomly sampled sentences from monolingual corpora in the same domain, but with no known parallel pairs. The parallel sentences used are the 2000 English-Icelandic sentence pairs made available as development data for the news translation task in WMT 2021.[3] The dev set for WMT 2021 contains 1000 sentences in each direction. The non-parallel sentences were randomly selected from Newscrawl 2018, and 2018 news texts sampled from the Icelandic Gigaword Corpus (Steingrímsson et al., 2018).

The texts were split into sentences. This resulted in two lists of $100,000$ sentences, English and Icelandic, with 2% of sentences in each list known to have a corresponding sentence in the other language.

We made a $40/60$ split, taking care that the true parallel sentence pairs were equally distributed between the splits. The smaller part was used as a development set and the larger part as a test set.

[3] Available at: `http://statmt.org/wmt21/translation-task.html`

3.2 CompWiki

We randomly selected 15 Wikipedia articles available in both Icelandic and English. The texts were split into sentences and the CLIR tool (see Section 4.1) used to obtain translation candidates for each sentence. These sentence pairs were manually evaluated and marked as parallel, partially parallel or non-parallel. Out of a total of $10,098$ sentences, 86 were marked parallel and 421 as partially parallel.

3.3 CompTrain

In order to gain some information on the kind of scores the two scoring methods give to non-parallel data, on the one hand, and parallel data, on the other hand, we compiled a dataset with $50,000$ randomly sampled pairs from the two monolingual corpora used for CompNews and added parallel sentences from the English–Icelandic ParIce corpus (Barkarson and Steingrímsson, 2019). We selected $2,500$ random sentence pairs from a development set published with the corpus and filtered all sentences that have a minimum length of six tokens. This resulted in $1,743$ sentence pairs, marked as positive data for a classifier. The resulting $51,743$ sentence pairs are scored in the same way we score the parallel sentence candidates (see Section 4.2) and used to train the classifier.

3.4 CompLex

FaDA, the cross-lingual information retrieval tool we use to obtain parallel pair candidates, requires a bilingual lexicon with lexical translation probabilities of words. It uses the lexicon to translate the query terms in the source language and searches these translated terms in the target-language index to retrieve the equivalent candidate sentences in the target language. It is described in more details in Section 4.1. As such a lexicon did not exist, we compiled it using a combination of approaches. We collected data that was available online, an English–Icelandic dictionary from Apertium (Brandt et al., 2011), Wiktionary entries and Wikipedia article titles. We obtained permission to use the bilingual ISLEX-dictionaries (Úlfarsdóttir, 2014), which go from Icelandic to five Nordic languages (Danish, Faroese, Finnish, Norwegian and Swedish) and used these to pivot to English using the aforementioned open dictionaries. We created word lists using word alignments to extract pairs from the ParIce corpus after lemmatizing both languages using SpaCy[4] for English and Nefnir (Ingólfsdóttir et al., 2019) and DIM (Bjarnadóttir et al., 2019) for Icelandic. We selected the most likely English equivalents for a list of Icelandic words using crosslingual word embeddings models based on Vecalign[5] (Thompson and Koehn, 2019). In addition, we translated both Icelandic words and words from the Nordic ISLEX-dictionaries, using models from OPUS-MT (Tiedemann and Thottingal, 2020). This resulted in a long list of word translation candidates which we then filtered using a threshold that required that each candidate was suggested by multiple sources. For each source word, we counted how many sources suggested that candidate and used the count to assign likelihood scores to the translations. This resulted in two files, an English–Icelandic lexicon with $140K$ entries and an Icelandic–English lexicon with $152K$ entries.

4 System Description

4.1 Sentence Alignment Using CLIR

We make use of an open source CLIR-based bilingual document alignment tool called *FaDA* (Lohar et al., 2016) in the first step of the alignment process. This tool is capable of aligning bilingual documents without the help of any MT system. In contrast, the MT-based alignment systems need additional time for translating all the source-language sentences into the target language. Therefore, *FaDA* reduces the computational overhead by skipping the translation process. As *FaDA* performs alignments at the document level, we consider each sentence separately and store it in a single document. Each document in our corpus therefore contains a single line of text. We then use the following functionalities of *FaDA* in our experiment.

(i) **Indexing**: First, we index both the source-language and the target-language documents,

(ii) ***Pseudo-query* construction**: Secondly, we construct a pseudo-query[6] from each source-language document using the terms selection procedure as shown in Equation (1).

$$\tau(t,d) = \lambda \frac{tf(t,d)}{len(d)} + (1-\lambda)\log(\frac{N}{df(t)}) \quad (1)$$

$tf(t,d)$ refers to the term frequency of a term t in a document d. $len(d)$ denotes the length of d, and N and $df(t)$ represents the total number of documents and the number of documents in which t occurs, respectively. $\tau(t,d)$ denotes the term-selection score which is a linear combination of the normalised term frequency of a term t in d, and the inverse document frequency (idf) of the term. The parameter λ controls the relative importance of tf and idf. We recommend the work of Lohar et al. (2016) for more details on *pseudo-query* construction.

(iii) **Word translation**: We then translate all the pseudo-query terms into the target-language with an English–Icelandic dictionary and search the translated query terms in the target-language index,

(iv) **Document retrieval**: Finally, we retrieve the *top-n*[7] target-language documents that are semantically equivalent to the source-language documents according to the IR-based retrieval.

4.2 Sentence Scoring

In the first step, the application of *FaDA* provides 10 (default value) target-language sentence candidates for each source-language sentence. This is

[4] https://spacy.io

[5] https://github.com/thompsonb/vecalign

[6] A *pseudo-query* is the modified version of the original query to improve the ranking of document retrieval. The terms in a pseudo-query are considered to be suitably representative of a document

[7] Note that $n = 10$ is the default value of n in *FaDA*. This means that the tool retrieves the top 10 candidate target-language documents by default.

done in both translation directions. We assume that most truly parallel sentences would be found in either direction and thus we create a subset of the *FaDA* outputs that contains an intersection of the candidate list for both directions. In order to test this hypotheses, we also create a union of both outputs when working with one of the test sets, *CompNews*.

We score our candidate lists using two methods, *LaBSE* (Feng et al., 2020), and *WAScore*, a word alignment-based score of our own device. Feng et al. (2020) show that *LaBSE* gives good results on the BUCC mining task when working with high-resource languages. However, the accuracy is reduced when working with less-resourced languages. In order to increase the accuracy of our extraction method, we use it together with another scoring mechanism that uses a very different approach. *WAScore* is calculated by collecting high precision word alignments using *CombAlign* (Steingrímsson et al., 2021). *CombAlign* uses a set of word alignment tools to perform the alignment and it has settings to aim for high precision or high recall, taking advantage of the fact that different alignment tools tend to make different guesses unless the alignment probabilities are high. We aim for high precision, thus removing most alignments that are not very likely to be correct. As this can be achieved by *CombAlign*, it makes WAScore an effective mechanism for measuring parallelism. *CombAlign* uses the following tools in our experiment; (i) *AWESoME* (Dou and Neubig, 2021), (ii) *eflomal* (Östling and Tiedemann, 2016), and (iii) *fast_align* (Dyer et al., 2013). WAScore is calculated for each sentence using Equation (2):

$$(s_a/s) * (t_a/t) \tag{2}$$

where s is the number of words in the source sentence and s_a is the number of source words that are aligned to some word in the target sentence, t is the number of words in the target sentence, and t_a is the number of target words that are aligned to some word in the source sentence.

With a set of highly likely alignments for each sentence pair, the WAScore tends to favour sentences of similar length as a much longer sentence on one side usually has proportionately few alignment edges on that side which lowers the score substantially. In contrast, if a shorter sentence on one side has all tokens aligned to a longer sentence on the other side, it can result in a reasonable score.

CompNews			
Set	Pr.	Rc.	F_1
Intersection	0.95	0.80	0.87
Union	0.92	0.86	0.86

Table 1: Precision, Recall F_1-measure and number of extracted sentences for a union and intersection of the *FaDA* output.

Such pairs are often partially parallel and using the *CompWiki* test set (Section 5.2) we see that our approach is suitable for extracting partially parallel pairs as well as truly parallel ones.

Finally, we use logistic regression to classify whether a sentence is parallel or not. All sentences accepted by the classifier are labelled as parallel sentences. The classifier is trained on the *CompTrain* training set, detailed earlier in Section 3.3.

5 Evaluation

We evaluate our system by calculating precision, recall and F1-scores using our (i) *CompNews* test set and (ii) *CompWiki* test set; and (iii) by training, testing and calculating BLEU scores for NMT systems, both with and without parallel sentences extracted from all Wikipedia articles that are available in both English and Icelandic.

5.1 Testing on News Data

The first experiment is on the *CompNews* test data, with the simple goal of extracting as many parallel sentence pairs as can be found from the two lists of $100K$ sentences in English and Icelandic. After running *FaDA* we obtain 10 candidates for each of the $100K$ sentences in each language. We create two different candidate sets, one by taking an intersection of both directions, en→is and is→en, and the other by taking a union of the two directions.

The intersection set contains $135K$ sentence pairs and an inspection of the set revealed that it

CompWiki			
Set	Pr.	Rc.	F_1
Parallel	0.39	0.90	0.54
+partially	0.84	0.33	0.47

Table 2: Precision, Recall and F_1-measure as measured when only looking at the sentence pairs marked as parallel in the test data, and when the partially parallel have been added to the desired output.

Wikipedia Training					
Training Data	Supplemental Sentences	TestEEA	TestEMA	TestOS	Combined
ParIce50K	0	9.0	9.0	1.6	8.1
ParIce50K+WikiMatrix	313,875	5.6	5.2	2.3	5.1
ParIce50K+Our approach	55,744	13.9	15.9	7.0	13.7

Table 3: BLEU scores for MT systems trained on parallel data and sentences extracted from comparable corpora.

included 1,693 of the total 2,000 known parallel sentence pairs in the data. The union set on the other hand had a total of 1.86 million pairs and 1,871 of the 2,000 correct sentence pairs.

We calculate LaBSE scores and WAScore for each of the candidates and apply our logistic regression classifier on the scores. The F-scores for both approaches were similar, but using the union data set obtains higher recall while using the intersection data obtains better precision. Table 1 shows the final results for the *CompNews* test set.

5.2 Testing on Wiki Data

The preparation of *CompWiki* was described in Section 3.2. It contains texts from 15 Wikipedia article pairs with a total of 10,098 sentence pairs. We score the sentences in the same way as discussed before, using LaBSE and WAScore, and run our classifier on the scores. 200 sentence pairs are deemed parallel by our classifier. 77 of them are marked parallel in the test set, 90 are marked partially parallel and 33 are marked non-parallel. As can be seen in Table 2, our method achieves high recall on the sentences marked parallel, and 84% of our systems output is either marked parallel or partially parallel.

5.3 Parallel Sentence Extraction and MT Training

We collect all texts from Wikipedia articles that are linked and available both in English and Icelandic. The collection contains 412,442 Icelandic sentences and 4,259,150 English sentences from 35,690 article pairs. In our setup, *FaDA* searches for the parallel candidates in the paired documents. The candidate pairs are then scored as before and classified as parallel or non-parallel. Our system yields 55,744 sentence pairs that are classified as parallel sentences.

There have been previous efforts in extracting parallel sentence from the Wikipedia corpus. One of the largest such efforts is the WikiMatrix project (Schwenk et al., 2021) that mined parallel sentences in 1,620 language pairs. When we compare the en–is language pair in WikiMatrix to the output of our system, the first obvious difference is that the WikiMatrix dataset has a lot more data, $314K$ sentence pairs compared to our $56K$. To compare the usefulness of the datasets, we trained an NMT system using Marian MT (Junczys-Dowmunt et al., 2018) in one direction, is→en, on $50K$ sentence pairs randomly sampled from the ParIce corpus and compared it to a system where WikiMatrix was added as supplemental data, and to a system where the results of our approach was used to supplement the ParIce data, using the same hyperparameters.

We compare BLEU scores for the different setups on a combination of three test sets (Barkarson and Steingrímsson, 2020), as well as on each of the test sets individually: TestEEA - containing sentence pairs from European Economic Area regulatory documents; TestEMA - containing sentence pairs from EMA drug descriptions; and TestOS - containing sentence pairs from OpenSubtitles. TestEEA and TestEMA are extracted from rather specialized texts, and generally have long sentences, while TestOS is from a rather open domain and tends to have shorter sentences. The test sets are used as filtered by Jónsson et al. (2020). All the sentence pairs in the test sets have been manually checked for correctness.

The fact that each of these three test sets are domain specific and that our NMT systems are not trained specifically on data from these domains, together with how small the training data sets are, results in low BLEU scores. But while the BLEU scores are quite low, the effect of our approach is evident.

We can see from Table 3 that when the WikiMatrix data is added to the $50K$ parallel sentences, the translation system trained on this augmented data set produces significantly lower BLEU scores as compared to the other two systems for the two test sets (TestEEA and TestEMA). However, it obtains higher BLEU scores than the baseline system (i.e, the system which is trained with only the $50K$ data) for the third test set (TestOS). In contrast, the system trained on the concatenation of the $50K$ sentence pairs and the data obtained from our approach significantly improves the BLEU scores for all the test sets, even though the number of sentence pairs in our data is less than 20% of the number of sentence pairs in WikiMatrix. This is most likely due to noise in WikiMatrix, as it has been shown that NMT is sensitive to noise in the training data (Khayrallah and Koehn, 2018).

Upon manual inspection of our data we see that our classifier accepted some sentence pairs even though they have a very low WAScore. We therefore train a number of NMT models using our data but apply thresholds for WAScore. As seen in Figure 2, the BLEU score rises when a low threshold is set, and then fluctuates when the threshold is raised, reaching the highest BLEU score for our combined test sets at a WAScore threshold of around 0.14. A WAScore of 0.14 means that if we have a pair of sentences containing ten tokens each, three tokens in one sentences align with four tokens in the other. If there are fewer alignments the sentence pair will not be accepted. At this threshold level we extract $34K$ parallel pairs to use for training. With further threshold filtering, we lose more beneficial data than detrimental data, and the BLEU score starts slipping down. This is an indicator of the usefulness of this scoring mechanism for MT training, showing that the score correlates with sentence pair parallelism, raising the BLEU score when it is used for filtering, and keeping it raised even though supplemental training data is reduced.

All of our data sets, for training and testing are available on Github, as well as a description of MarianMT training setup[8].

6 Conclusions and Future work

We have shown that our method, combining cross-lingual information extraction, contextualized embeddings and word alignments, is efficient at finding parallel segments in comparable corpora. Furthermore we introduce WAScore, a metric of translational equivalence based on high-precision word alignments, and show that as well as being a useful part of a binary classifier, it can be used effectively to filter out detrimental segments from parallel corpora. Finally, we publish two new test sets for extracting parallel sentences from comparable corpora, an automatically generated English–Icelandic lexicon with probability scores and a set of automatically extracted parallel segments that we show are useful for training MT systems.

When testing on the *CompWiki* test set we saw that while our method is efficient in finding parallel segments in comparable corpora, it also selects partially parallel segments. Although these segments seem to have information useful for training MT

[8]`https://github.com/steinst/bucc2021-en-is`

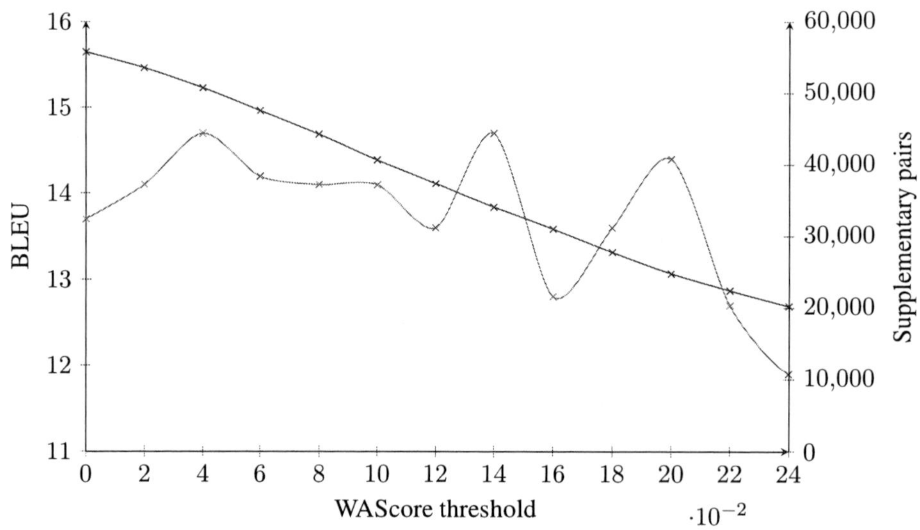

Figure 2: BLEU score for MarianMT models training with supplementary data, with different WAScore thresholds over the combined test sets.

systems, it is difficult to know to what extent they are useful and when they may become detrimental. For this reason, we plan to study these kinds of data further and investigate how they affect translation quality of an NMT system trained on it. Based on that, we want to explore more sophisticated ways to segment or concatenate alignment candidates in order to be able to build a data set that only contains segment pairs that are useful for training MT systems. There is previous work on parallel fragment extraction using word alignments (Yeong et al., 2019), and we will use their approach as a baseline to proceed further.

While the combination of the two scores used to measure the quality of the sentence pairs resulted in a list of sentence pairs that we show are useful for MT training, it still contains pairs that are detrimental, as shown by the simple filtering based on WAScore threshold. Other parallel sentence pairs may also remain to be found in the Wikipedia data. In order to improve our approach, more scores could be added to our classifier. While we opted to use raw LaBSE cosine similarity scores, shown by (Feng et al., 2020) to be more accurate than cosine similarity scores from other models, the margin-based ratio score proposed by Artetxe and Schwenk (2019a) has also been shown to be very effective for this task. Other scores to consider could include BLEU or ChrF (Popović, 2015), although they need reasonably good MT systems to be useful, margin-based cosine distance (Artetxe and Schwenk, 2019a), or Mahalanobis distance (Mahalanobis, 1936) as described in Littell et al. (2018). Doing an ablation study on the scores could help determine which are the most useful. Working with these scores, a comparison of applying different classifiers while using the same scoring mechanisms may be helpful. It is also to be noted that we extracted only 10 target-language candidate pairs in the first step, which is the default value used in *FaDA* as it gave optimal performance in their work. It also has the benefit of reducing the computational complexity in the next steps. However, we also plan to explore other higher values of candidate extraction in future and to investigate how it affects the overall system performance. Finally, we plan to conduct our experiments on other language pairs.

Acknowledgements

This work is supported by the Language Technology Programme for Icelandic 2019-2023, funded by the Icelandic government, and by the ADAPT Centre for Digital Content Technology which is funded under the Science Foundation Ireland (SFI) Research Centres Programme (Grant No. 13/RC/2106) and is co-funded under the European Regional Development Fund.

References

Haithem Afli, Loïc Barrault, and Holger Schwenk. 2015. Building and using multimodal comparable corpora for machine translation. *Natural Language Engineering*, 22(4):603 – 625.

Thierry Etchegoyhen Andoni Azpeitia and Eva Martínez Garcia. 2018. Extracting parallel sentences from comparable corpora with stacc variants. In *Proceedings of the Eleventh International Conference on Language Resources and Evaluation (LREC 2018)*, Paris, France.

Mikel Artetxe, Gorka Labaka, and Eneko Agirre. 2018. Unsupervised Statistical Machine Translation. In *Proceedings of the 2018 Conference on Empirical Methods in Natural Language Processing*, pages 3632–3642, Brussels, Belgium.

Mikel Artetxe and Holger Schwenk. 2019a. Margin-based Parallel Corpus Mining with Multilingual Sentence Embeddings. In *Proceedings of the 57th Annual Meeting of the Association for Computational Linguistics*, pages 3197–3203, Florence, Italy.

Mikel Artetxe and Holger Schwenk. 2019b. Massively Multilingual Sentence Embeddings for Zero-Shot Cross-Lingual Transfer and Beyond. *Transactions of the Association for Computational Linguistics*, 7:597–610.

Andoni Azpeitia, Thierry Etchegoyhen, and Eva Martínez Garcia. 2017. Weighted set-theoretic alignment of comparable sentences. In *Proceedings of the 10th Workshop on Building and Using Comparable Corpora*, pages 41–45, Vancouver, Canada.

Starkaður Barkarson and Steinþór Steingrímsson. 2019. Compiling and Filtering ParIce: An English-Icelandic Parallel Corpus. In *Proceedings of the 22nd Nordic Conference on Computational Linguistics*, pages 140–145, Turku, Finland.

Starkaður Barkarson and Steinþór Steingrímsson. 2020. ParIce dev/test/train splits 20.05. CLARIN-IS.

Kristín Bjarnadóttir, Kristín Ingibjörg Hlynsdóttir, and Steinþór Steingrímsson. 2019. DIM: The Database of Icelandic Morphology. In *Proceedings of the 22nd Nordic Conference on Computational Linguistics*, pages 146–154, Turku, Finland.

Martha Dís Brandt, Hrafn Loftsson, Hlynur Sigurþórsson, and Francis M. Tyers. 2011. Apertium-IceNLP: A rule-based Icelandic to English machine translation system. In *Proceedings of the 15th Annual conference of the European Association for Machine Translation*, pages 217–224, Leuven, Belgium.

Chenhui Chu, Toshiaki Nakazawa, and Sadao Kurohashi. 2015. Integrated Parallel Sentence and Fragment Extraction from Comparable Corpora: A Case Study on Chinese–Japanese Wikipedia. *ACM Transactions on Asian and Low-Resource Language Information Processing*, 15(2).

Zi-Yi Dou and Graham Neubig. 2021. Word Alignment by Fine-tuning Embeddings on Parallel Corpora. In *Proceedings of the 16th Conference of the European Chapter of the Association for Computational Linguistics: Main Volume*, pages 2112–2128, Online.

Chris Dyer, Victor Chahuneau, and Noah A. Smith. 2013. A Simple, Fast, and Effective Reparameterization of IBM Model 2. In *Proceedings of the 2013 Conference of the North American Chapter of the Association for Computational Linguistics: Human Language Technologies*, pages 644–648, Atlanta, Georgia.

Fangxiaoyu Feng, Yin-Fei Yang, Daniel Matthew Cer, N. Arivazhagan, and Wei Wang. 2020. Language-agnostic bert sentence embedding. *ArXiv*, abs/2007.01852.

Viktor Hangya and Alexander Fraser. 2019. Unsupervised Parallel Sentence Extraction with Parallel Segment Detection Helps Machine Translation. In *Proceedings of the 57th Annual Meeting of the Association for Computational Linguistics*, pages 1224–1234, Florence, Italy.

Svanhvít Lilja Ingólfsdóttir, Hrafn Loftsson, Jón Friðrik Daðason, and Kristín Bjarnadóttir. 2019. Nefnir: A high accuracy lemmatizer for Icelandic. In *Proceedings of the 22nd Nordic Conference on Computational Linguistics*, pages 310–315, Turku, Finland.

Haukur Páll Jónsson, Haukur Barri Símonarson, Vésteinn Snæbjarnarson, Steinþór Steingrímsson, and Hrafn Loftsson. 2020. Experimenting with different machine translation models in medium-resource settings. In *Text, Speech, and Dialogue - 23rd International Conference, TSD 2020, Brno, Czech Republic, September 8-11, 2020, Proceedings*, volume 12284 of *Lecture Notes in Computer Science*, pages 95–103.

Marcin Junczys-Dowmunt, Kenneth Heafield, Hieu Hoang, Roman Grundkiewicz, and Anthony Aue. 2018. Marian: Cost-effective High-Quality Neural Machine Translation in C++. In *Proceedings of the 2nd Workshop on Neural Machine Translation and Generation*, pages 129–135, Melbourne, Australia.

Akbar Karimi, Ebrahim Ansari, and Bahram Sadeghi Bigham. 2018. Extracting an English-Persian parallel corpus from comparable corpora. In *Proceedings of the Eleventh International Conference on Language Resources and Evaluation (LREC 2018)*, pages 3477–3482, Miyazaki, Japan.

Shahram Khadivi and Hermann Ney. 2005. Automatic Filtering of Bilingual Corpora for Statistical Machine Translation. In *Natural Language Processing and Information Systems*, pages 263–274, Berlin, Heidelberg. Springer Berlin Heidelberg.

Huda Khayrallah and Philipp Koehn. 2018. On the Impact of Various Types of Noise on Neural Machine Translation. In *Proceedings of the 2nd Workshop on Neural Machine Translation and Generation*, pages 74–83, Melbourne, Australia.

Yunsu Kim, Miguel Graça, and Hermann Ney. 2020. When and Why is Unsupervised Neural Machine Translation Useless? In *Proceedings of the 22nd Annual Conference of the European Association for Machine Translation*, pages 35–44, Lisboa, Portugal.

Guillaume Lample, Myle Ott, Alexis Conneau, Ludovic Denoyer, and Marc'Aurelio Ranzato. 2018. Phrase-Based & Neural Unsupervised Machine Translation. In *Proceedings of the 2018 Conference on Empirical Methods in Natural Language Processing*, pages 5039–5049, Brussels, Belgium.

Wang Ling, Luís Marujo, Chris Dyer, Alan W. Black, and Isabel Trancoso. 2014. Crowdsourcing High-Quality Parallel Data Extraction from Twitter. In *Proceedings of the Ninth Workshop on Statistical Machine Translation*, pages 426–436, Baltimore, Maryland, USA.

Patrick Littell, Samuel Larkin, Darlene Stewart, Michel Simard, Cyril Goutte, and Chi-kiu Lo. 2018. Measuring sentence parallelism using mahalanobis distances: The NRC unsupervised submissions to the WMT18 parallel corpus filtering shared task. In *Proceedings of the Third Conference on Machine Translation: Shared Task Papers*, pages 900–907, Belgium, Brussels.

Pintu Lohar, Debasis Ganguly, Haithem Afli, Andy Way, and Gareth J. F. Jones. 2016. Fada: Fast document aligner using word embedding. *The Prague Bulletin of Mathematical Linguistics*, 106:169–179.

Jun Lu, Xin Ge, Yangbin Shi, and Yuqi Zhang. 2020. Alibaba Submission to the WMT20 Parallel Corpus Filtering Task. In *Proceedings of the Fifth Conference on Machine Translation*, pages 979–984, Online.

Prasanta Chandra Mahalanobis. 1936. On the generalized distance in statistics. *Proceedings of the National Institute of Sciences (Calcutta)*, 2:49–55.

Robert Östling and Jörg Tiedemann. 2016. Efficient word alignment with Markov Chain Monte Carlo. *Prague Bulletin of Mathematical Linguistics*, 106:125–146.

Kishore Papineni, Salim Roukos, Todd Ward, and Wei-Jing Zhu. 2002. Bleu: a Method for Automatic Evaluation of Machine Translation. In *Proceedings of the 40th Annual Meeting of the Association for Computational Linguistics*, pages 311–318, Philadelphia, Pennsylvania, USA.

Maja Popović. 2015. chrF: character n-gram F-score for automatic MT evaluation. In *Proceedings of the Tenth Workshop on Statistical Machine Translation*, pages 392–395, Lisbon, Portugal.

Gowtham Ramesh, Sumanth Doddapaneni, Aravinth Bheemaraj, Mayank Jobanputra, AK Raghavan, Ajitesh Sharma, Sujit Sahoo, Harshita Diddee, J. Mahalakshmi, Divyanshu Kakwani, Navneet Kumar, Aswin Pradeep, Kumar Deepak, Vivek Raghavan, Anoop Kunchukuttan, Pratyush Kumar, and M. Khapra. 2021. Samanantar: The Largest Publicly Available Parallel Corpora Collection for 11 Indic Languages. *ArXiv*, abs/2104.05596.

Holger Schwenk. 2018. Filtering and Mining Parallel Data in a Joint Multilingual Space. In *Proceedings of the 56th Annual Meeting of the Association for Computational Linguistics (Volume 2: Short Papers)*, pages 228–234, Melbourne, Australia.

Holger Schwenk, Vishrav Chaudhary, Shuo Sun, Hongyu Gong, and Francisco Guzmán. 2021. WikiMatrix: Mining 135M Parallel Sentences in 1620 Language Pairs from Wikipedia. In *Proceedings of the 16th Conference of the European Chapter of the Association for Computational Linguistics: Main Volume*, pages 1351–1361, Online.

Steinþór Steingrímsson, Sigrún Helgadóttir, Eiríkur Rögnvaldsson, Starkaður Barkarson, and Jón Guðnason. 2018. Risamálheild: A Very Large Icelandic Text Corpus. In *Proceedings of the Eleventh International Conference on Language Resources and Evaluation (LREC 2018)*, pages 4361–4366, Miyazaki, Japan.

Steinþór Steingrímsson, Hrafn Loftsson, and Andy Way. 2021. CombAlign: a Tool for Obtaining High-Quality Word Alignments. In *Proceedings of the 23rd Nordic Conference on Computational Linguistics (NoDaLiDa)*, pages 64–73, Reykjavik, Iceland (Online).

Sara Stymne, Christian Hardmeier, Jörg Tiedemann, and Joakim Nivre. 2013. Tunable Distortion Limits and Corpus Cleaning for SMT. In *Proceedings of the Eighth Workshop on Statistical Machine Translation*, pages 225–231, Sofia, Bulgaria.

Brian Thompson and Philipp Koehn. 2019. Vecalign: Improved Sentence Alignment in Linear Time and Space. In *Proceedings of the 2019 Conference on Empirical Methods in Natural Language Processing and the 9th International Joint Conference on Natural Language Processing (EMNLP-IJCNLP)*, pages 1342–1348, Hong Kong, China.

Jörg Tiedemann and Santhosh Thottingal. 2020. OPUS-MT – Building open translation services for the World. In *Proceedings of the 22nd Annual Conference of the European Association for Machine Translation*, pages 479–480, Lisboa, Portugal.

Þórdís Úlfarsdóttir. 2014. ISLEX — a Multilingual Web Dictionary. In *Proceedings of the Ninth International Conference on Language Resources and Evaluation (LREC'14)*, pages 2820–2825, Reykjavik, Iceland.

Krzysztof Wolk, Emilia Rejmund, and Krzysztof Marasek. 2016. Multi-domain machine translation enhancements by parallel data extraction from comparable corpora. In Ewa Gruszczyńska and Agnieszka Leńko-Szymańska, editors, *Polish-Language Parallel Corpora*, pages 157–179. Instytut Lingwistyki Stosowanej, Warsaw, Poland.

Yin-Lai Yeong, Tien-Ping Tan, and Keng Hoon Gan. 2019. A Hybrid of Sentence-Level Approach and Fragment-Level Approach of Parallel Text Extraction from Comparable Text. *Procedia Computer Science*, 161:406–414.

Ieva Zariņa, Pēteris Ņikiforovs, and Raivis Skadiņš. 2015. Word Alignment Based Parallel Corpora Evaluation and Cleaning Using Machine Learning Techniques. In *Proceedings of the 18th Annual Conference of the European Association for Machine Translation*, pages 185–192, Antalya, Turkey.

Pierre Zweigenbaum, Serge Sharoff, and Reinhard Rapp. 2016. Towards Preparation of the Second BUCC Shared Task: Detecting Parallel Sentences in Comparable Corpora. In *Proceedings of the Ninth Workshop on Building and Using Comparable Corpora*, pages 38–43, Portorož, Slovenia. ELDA.

Syntax-aware Transformers for Neural Machine Translation: The Case of Text to Sign Gloss Translation

Santiago Egea Gómez
Universitat Pompeu Fabra
santiago.egea@upf.edu

Euan McGill
Universitat Pompeu Fabra
euan.mcgill@upf.edu

Horacio Saggion
Universitat Pompeu Fabra
horacio.saggion@upf.edu

Abstract

It is well-established that the preferred mode of communication of the deaf and hard of hearing (DHH) community are Sign Languages (SLs), but they are considered low resource languages where natural language processing technologies are of concern. In this paper we study the problem of text to SL gloss Machine Translation (MT) using Transformer-based architectures. Despite the significant advances of MT for spoken languages in the recent couple of decades, MT is in its infancy when it comes to SLs. We enrich a Transformer-based architecture aggregating syntactic information extracted from a dependency parser to word-embeddings. We test our model on a well-known dataset showing that the syntax-aware model obtains performance gains in terms of MT evaluation metrics.

1 Introduction

Access to information is a human right and crossing language barriers is essential for global information exchange and unobstructed, fair communication. However, we are still far from the goal of making information accessible to all a reality. The World Health Organisation (WHO) reports that there are some 466 million people in the world today with disabling hearing loss[1]; moreover, it is estimated that this number will double by 2050. According to the World Federation of the Deaf (WFD), over 70 million people are deaf and communicate primarily via a sign language (SL).

It is well-established that the preferred mode of communication of the deaf and hard of hearing (DHH) community are SLs (Stoll et al., 2020), but they are considered *extremely* low resource languages (Moryossef et al., 2021), and lag further behind in terms of the provision of language technologies available to DHH people. 150 SLs have been classified around the world (Eberhard et al., 2021) while there may be upwards of 400 according to SIL International[2]. Creating accessible-to-all technological solutions may also mitigate the effect of more variable reading literacy rate in the DHH community (Berke et al., 2018). The written language is usually the ambient spoken language in the geographical area signers are found (e.g. English in the British Sign Language area), and providing resources in native SL could benefit the provision and uptake of sign language technology.

Machine translation (MT) (Koehn, 2009) is a core technique for reducing language barriers that has advanced, and seen many breakthroughs since it began in the 1950s (Johnson et al., 2017), to reach quality levels comparable to humans (Hassan et al., 2018). Despite the significant advances of MT for spoken languages in the recent couple of decades, MT is in its infancy when it comes to SLs.

The output of MT between spoken languages tends to be text, but there are further considerations for researchers doing Sign Language translation (SLT). Full writing systems exist for SL (e.g. HamNoSys (Hanke, 2004), SiGML (Zwitserlood et al., 2004)), but are not always the output or used at all in SLT. SL glosses are a lexeme-based representation of signs where classifier predicates, manual and non-manual cues (Porta et al., 2014) are distilled into a lexical representation, usually in the ambient spoken language. The articulators in SLs include hand configuration and trajectory, facial articulators including lip position and eyebrow configuration, and spatial articulation including eye gaze and body position (Mukushev et al., 2020) - all used to convey meaning. Glosses, and the Text2Gloss process, are an essential step in the MT

[1] https://www.who.int/news-room/fact-sheets/detail/deafness-and-hearing-loss

[2] https://www.sil.org/sign-languages

Proceedings of 14th Workshop on Building and Using Comparable Corpora in conjunction with RANLP-2021, pages 18–27, held online, 6 September 2021.
https://doi.org/10.26615/978-954-452-076-2_004

pipeline between spoken and sign languages - even though they are considered a flawed representation which hinder the extraction of meaning by some researchers (Yin and Read, 2020). Although some current approaches to SL translation follow an end-to-end paradigm, translating into glosses offers an intermediate representation which could drive the generation of the actual virtual signs (e.g. by an avatar) (Almeida et al., 2015; López-Ludeña et al., 2014). A growing number of researchers (Jantunen et al., 2021) have been using innovative methods to leverage the limited supply of SL gloss corpora and resources for SL technology.

In spite of the impressive results achieved by Neural Machine Translation (NMT) when massive parallel data-sets are available for training using just token level information, recent research (Armengol Estapé and Ruiz Costa-Jussà, 2021) shows that morphological and syntactic information extracted from linguistic processors can be of help for out-of-domain machine translation or rich morphology languages.

In this work, we make transformer models for NMT *'syntax-aware'* - where syntactic information embeddings are included as well as word embeddings in the encoder part of the model. The rationale behind including syntactic embeddings draws from the success of word embeddings improving natural language processing tasks including syntactic parsing itself (Socher et al., 2013), and from context-sensitive embeddings pioneered in transformer models (Vaswani et al., 2017; Devlin et al., 2019; Liu et al., 2020). We posit that encoding syntactic information will in turn boost the performance of Text2Gloss as we show with our experimental results.

The rest of the paper is organised in the following way: in the next section we briefly introduce the project in the context of which this work is being carried out. Then, in Section 3, we present related work on SL translation and background on NMT and in Section 4 we describe the NMT architecture we use in our experiments. In Section 5 we describe the experimental methodology including data and evaluation metrics while in Section 6 we present quantitative results. Section 7 analyses the results while Section 8 closes the paper and discusses further work which could expand this avenue of research.

2 The SignON project

SignON[3] is a Horizon 2020 project which aims to develop a communication service that translates between sign and spoken (in both text and audio modalities) languages and caters for the communication needs between DHH and hearing individuals (Saggion et al., 2021). Currently, human interpreters are the main medium for sign-to-spoken, spoken-to-sign and sign-to-sign language translation. The availability and cost of these professionals is often a limiting factor in communication between signers and non-signers. The SignON communication service will translate between sign and spoken languages, bridging language gaps when professional interpretation is unavailable. A key piece of this project is the server which will host the translation engine, which imposes demanding requirements in terms of latency and efficiency.

3 Related Work

The bottleneck to creating SL technology primarily lies in the training data available, such as from existing corpora and lexica. Certain corpora may be overly domain-specific (San-Segundo et al., 2010), containing only sentence fragments or example signs as part of a lexicon (Cabeza et al., 2016), have little variation in individual signers or the framing of the signer in 3D space (Nunnari et al., 2021), or simply too small in size to be applied to large neural models alone (Jantunen et al., 2021).

The next section describes current methods to mitigate the data-scarcity problem, and state-of-the-art models and studies with sign language gloss data - including Text2Gloss, Gloss2Text, and efforts towards end-to-end (E2E) SLT.

3.1 Transformer models for NMT

Transformer architecture has been successful in covering a large amount of language pairs with great accuracy in MT tasks, most notably in models such as BART (Lewis et al., 2020) and mBART (Liu et al., 2020). mT5 (Xue et al., 2021) also performs well with an even larger set of languages, many of which are considered low-resource. These models are also highly adaptable to other NLP tasks by means of finetuning (Lewis et al., 2020). In addition, recent work has shown that transformer models including embeddings with linguistic information in a low-resource language pair improve model

[3]`https://signon-project.eu/`

Table 1: T2G production examples

Spoken	Später breiten sich aber nebel oder hochnebelfelder aus (EN) Later, however, fog or high-fog fields are widening
Gloss	ABER IM-VERLAUF NEBEL HOCH NEBEL IX[4] (EN) BUT IN-COURSE FOG HIGH FOG IX

performance by 1.2 BLEU score (Armengol Estapé and Ruiz Costa-Jussà, 2021) over a baseline - and when using arbitrary features derived from neural models (Sennrich and Haddow, 2016). Their 'Factored Transformer' model inserts embeddings for lemmas, part-of-speech tags, lexical dependencies, and morphological features in the encoder of their attentional encoder-decoder architecture.

In this work, a syntax-aware transformer model is proposed for Text2Gloss translation - one step in the SLT pipeline. Although current steps towards E2E SLT using transformer-based NMT systems look promising (Nunnari et al., 2021), using glosses as an intermediate representation still improve performance even in these state-of-the-art systems (Camgoz et al., 2020; Yin and Read, 2020). Our model exploits lexical dependency information to assist in learning the intrinsic grammatical rules that involves translating from text to glosses. Unlike other works, we consider model simplicity a key feature to fulfil efficiency requirements in the SignON Project. Thus, we applied an easy aggregation scheme to inject syntactic information to the model and chose a relatively simple neural architecture. Using only lexical dependency features also allows us to examine the impact of this individual linguistic feature on model performance.

4 System Overview: A Syntax-aware Transformer for Text2Gloss

Our model is an Encoder-Decoder architecture which consists of augmenting the input embeddings to the Encoder via including lexical dependency information. As can be noted from Table 1, gloss production from spoken text is essentially based on word permutations, stemming and deletions. In many cases, those transformations depend on the syntactical functions of word, for example determiners are always removed to produce glosses. Consequently, we believe that word dependency tags might assist in modelling syntactic rules which are intrinsic in gloss production.

Importantly, our Text2Gloss model has been developed considering the efficiency requirements demanded for the SignON Project. Therefore, the size of the architecture has been selected to produce accurate but also lightweight translations. Figure 1 shows the different modules composing our system.

The neural architecture employed is based on multi-attention layers (Vaswani et al., 2017), which has produced excellent results when modelling long input sequences. More specifically, the Encoder and Decoder are composed by three multi-attention layers with four attention heads. The internal dimensions for the fully connected network are set to 1024 and the output units to 512. The Encoder transforms inputs to latent vectors, whilst the Decoder produces word probabilities from the encoded latent representations.

Our system augments the discriminative power of the embeddings inputted to the Encoder by aggregating syntactic information to word embeddings. Unlike (Armengol Estapé and Ruiz Costa-Jussà, 2021) (which added encoders to manage injected features), we integrate an additional table that contains the vector embeddings for the syntactic tags. The word and syntax embeddings are sum up producing an aggregated embedding that is input to the Encoder. Both tables were set to have a vector length of 512.

To accommodate input text to the neural model, we process it employing subword tokenisation and dependency tags are produced using the model *de_core_news_sm* available in the *spaCy*[5] library. The dependency tags we incorporate are from the TIGER dependency bank (Albert et al., 2003), included in the German model, and designed specifically to categorise words in German (Brants et al., 2004). An example of these tags with a German sentence is shown in Figure 2. Then, word and syntax tokens were aligned with the corresponding words as shown in Figure 1. For the tokeniser, a Sentence Piece model (Kudo and Richardson, 2018) was trained using only the training corpus with a vocabulary size of 3000, keeping some tokens for control.

Regarding the training, Adam optimiser with a learning rate of 10^{-5} and a batch size of 64 was applied to optimise Cross Categorical Entropy for 500 epochs. Text generation was carried out using

[4]IX gloss indicates that the signer needs to point to something or someone.

[5]`https://spacy.io/`

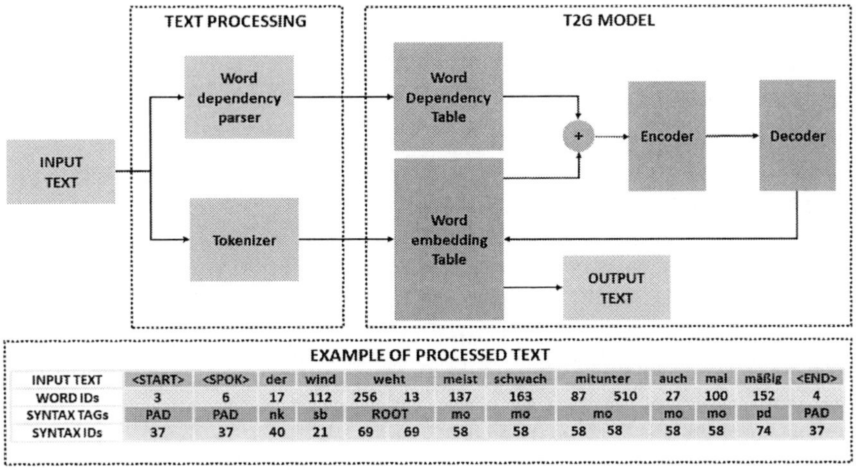

Figure 1: Syntax-Aware Text2Gloss model

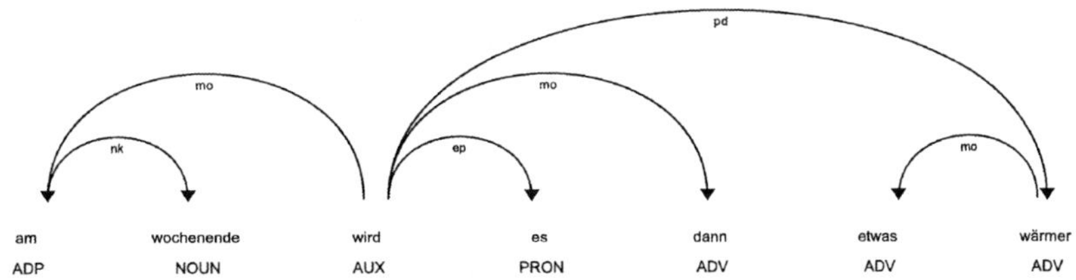

Figure 2: Lexical dependency tree diagram of the sentence "On the weekend it gets a little warmer". Key to tags: ep = expletive *es*, mo = modifier, nk = noun kernel element, pd = predicate

Beam Search Decoding with 5 beams.

5 Methods & Materials

In this section, we present the methods and materials used in this research. Firstly, we introduce the dataset used and performance metrics and other implementation details are described.

5.1 Dataset: RWTH-PHOENIX-2014-T

The parallel corpus selected for our experiments is the *RWTH-PHOENIX-2014-T* (Camgoz et al., 2018). It is publicly available [6], and is widely-adopted for SLT research. This dataset contains images, and transcriptions in German text and German Sign Language (DGS) glosses of weather forecasting news from a public TV station. The large vocabulary (1,066 different signs) and number of signers (nine) make this dataset promising for SLT research, in an albeit limited semantic domain. In this study, we only consider the text and gloss transcriptions.

[6] https://www-i6.informatik.rwth-aachen.de/~koller/RWTH-PHOENIX-2014-T/

Table 2: Data partitions Information

	#Samples	#Words	#Glosses
Train	7096	2887	1085
Dev	519	951	393
Test	642	1001	411

The authors included *development* and *test* partitions in their dataset with unseen patterns in the training data. We used the *development* subset to control overfitting and performances are reported on the *test* subset. The information about the different subsets included in RWTH-PHOENIX-2014-T is presented in Table 2.

5.2 Performance Metrics

In order to fairly evaluate our approach, we have selected performance metrics that are extensively used in NMT. Consequently, the metrics used are introduced below:

Translation Edit Rate (TER): TER (Snover et al., 2006) measures the quality of system translations by counting the number of text edits needed to transform the produced test into the reference.

SacreBLEU: SacreBLEU (Post, 2018) is a very popular metric for NMT. It facilitates the implementation of BLEU (Papineni et al., 2002) and standardises input schemes to the metric by means of tokenisation and normalisation. This in turn makes comparing scores from other works more directly comparable and straightforward. BLEU aims to correlate a *'human-level'* judgement of quality by using a reference translation as part of its calculation.

ROUGE-L F1: ROUGE-L (Lin, 2004) was primarily conceived for evaluating text summarisation models, however it has become popular for other NLP tasks. It measures the longest sequence in common between the given reference and model output sentence, without pre-defining an N-Gram length. We report the F1 score to measure model accuracy, as also seen in other works on this dataset (Camgoz et al., 2018; Yin and Read, 2020).

METEOR: METEOR (Banerjee and Lavie, 2005) is a metric for MT evaluation based on unigram matching. This metric is based on unigram-precision and recall to consider word alignments, with recall having more influence on the score. It is considered to have a higher correlation with human judgement than BLEU.

Generation time: Finally, the generation time is reported to assess our system in terms of computational efficiency. It is reported in seconds for each model.

5.3 Implementation Details

The experiments reported here were carried out using *Tensorflow* as Deep Learning framework. The Embedding Tables, Encoder and Decoder implementations were inherited from the *HuggingFace-transformers* library [7] and *spaCy* was employed to produce word-dependency features. Finally, NLTK and other third-party code[8, 9, 10] was used to compute the performance metrics adopted here. We make our code publicly available at GitHub[11].

6 Results

Here, we present the results from our experiment. As the objective of this research is evaluating the benefits of injecting syntactic information for Text2Gloss translation, we compare two models with the same architecture: One including, and one not including lexical dependency information. Those models are denoted as Syntax and No-Syntax respectively in this and subsequent sections.

6.1 Performance vs Epochs

Figure 3 presents the evolution of the performance metrics after each 5 training epochs while the models are being trained. It is apparent that including the syntactic information brings notable benefits for the most of the metrics adopted, with the exception of METEOR.

Focusing on sacreBLEU score, the Syntax model produces substantially better translations after 80 training epochs. After this point, the models converge and the difference in the sacreBLEU score between the models becomes more evident. Namely, the greatest difference between both models happens at epoch 165, when Syntax model produces a sacreBLEU 5.7 points higher than No-Syntax.

As for TER, the differences between curves are more remarkable. Syntax model produces TER scores notably better than the No-syntax, the score becomes stable after 95 epochs and tends to reduce its oscillations. At this point Syntax model outperforms the No-syntax model in around 0.15 for TER.

According to the ROUGE-L (F1-score) obtained, we also observe a slight improvement of Syntax model over No-syntax, although this increase is not clear until epoch 150. In this case the differences are not as clear as the metrics already observed, but it implies enhancements higher that 0.01 for this metric.

The METEOR score is the only metric that does not improve when syntactic information is included. In this regard, the No-syntax model produced better

[7] `https://huggingface.co/transformers/`

[8] `https://github.com/BramVanroy/pyter`

[9] `https://github.com/mjpost/sacrebleu`

[10] `https://github.com/google/seq2seq/blob/master/seq2seq/metrics/rouge.py`

[11] `https://github.com/LaSTUS-TALN-UPF/Syntax-Aware-Transformer-Text2Gloss`

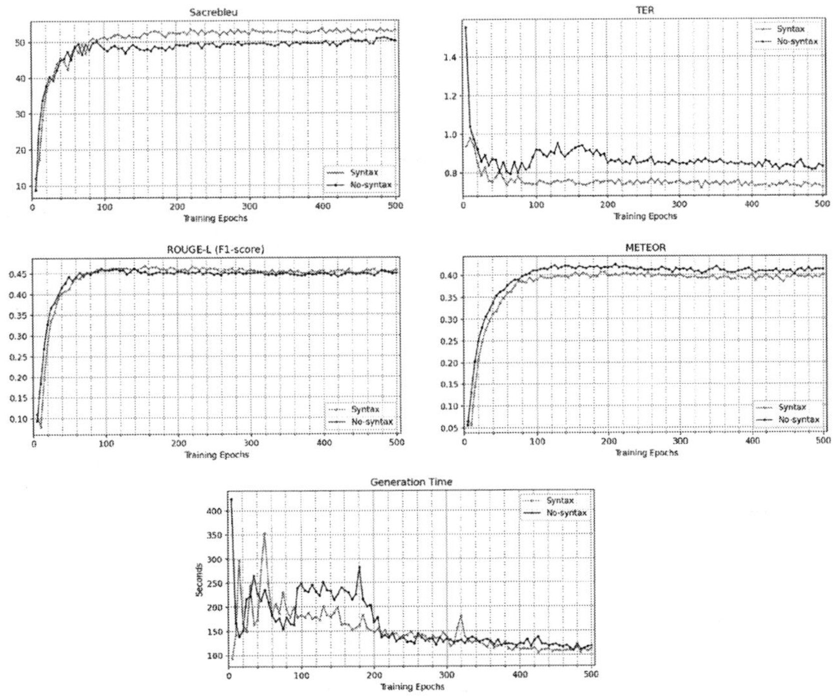

Figure 3: Performance Metrics evolution during training.

translations in terms of this score for all the whole training phase. When the models converge after 100 epochs, the greatest difference between models happens at epoch 350 when No-syntax overcomes the Syntax model by 0.029 points. It is also remarkable that the differences between models are not higher than 0.015 for most of the points after convergence. The reason why No-Syntax produces a slightly better METEOR than Syntax might be the fact that METEOR benefits unigram recall and the No-Syntax model tends to repeat words, as we show in next Section. Nonetheless, we will further analyse this observation in future research.

Finally, as efficiency is one of the goals of our project, we turn to generation time. From the Generation Time curves shown in Figure 3, we can observe that injecting syntactic information does not lead to marked generation time increases. We include the extra time necessary to produce the lexical dependency tags. In the case of the training subset, the tagging process took around 20.9 seconds, this processing time constitutes an increase of 2.95 milliseconds per sentence compared to not using syntax tags. Regarding the test subset, the tag process lasted 3.23 seconds in total, which is not a marked increase considering the total generation times and that Syntax is until 60 seconds faster than No-syntax (this is the case for 155 to 180 epochs). The cause behind the great differences in generation times might be that Beam Search decoding produces more precise hypotheses and needs less decoding iterations when syntax tags are employed.

6.2 Best-performing points

From the previous analysis, we have identified the points in which the neural models converge and where high variation is not present in the metric curves. In this section, we focused on the points in which the metrics reach their maximum values after convergence point, which is located around epoch 100. Table 3 shows the best-performing values for all metrics.

From Table 3, we observe that the Syntax model reaches its maximum values with less epochs than No-syntax. This observation indicates that syntactic information also might benefit the neural model learning leading to shorter training times. Another observation is that the most of metrics are improved by injecting syntactic information, with the exception of METEOR.

Table 3: Best scores for the models. This table contains the maximum values for all metrics after convergence. The values between parenthesis denotes the epoch in which those values are produced.

	SacreBLEU↑	TER↓	ROUGE-L (F1-score)↑	METEOR↑
Syntax	53.52 (400)	0.722 (330)	0.467 (115)	0.407 (190)
No-syntax	51.06 (485)	0.814 (485)	0.461 (140)	0.424 (210)
Diff	2.46 (85)	-0.092 (155)	0.006 (35)	-0.017 (-20)

7 Discussion

In the previous section, we have described quantitatively the results produced from our selected metrics. Additionally, this section presents a qualitative analysis of the benefits produced for Text2Gloss translation including lexical information in the transformer model. Table 4 contains two examples on how both models produce glosses at different training points.

As can be noted in both examples, the No-syntax model needs more epochs to produce coherent translations and tends to repeat some patterns leading to corrupted outputs in some cases. This effect is quite remarkable in the second example, for which No-syntax retains repeating patterns after 100 epochs while Syntax produces more coherent translations. This fact might lead to the No-Syntax model obtaining a slightly higher METEOR than Syntax (see 6.1), while Syntax substantially outperformed its competitor in terms of Sacrebleu.

The fast-learning capacity exhibited by the Syntax model could be advantageous for our project, since domain-adaptation is an expected feature for the system under development. Also, we have shown that injecting syntactic information to the encoder enables more accurate models without wholesale architecture modifications. The feature injection could be extended to other lexical features, such as Part-of-Speech tags, via integrating a new embedding table.

8 Conclusion

In this paper we present a syntax-aware transformer for Text2Gloss. To make the model syntax-aware we inject word dependency tags to augment the discriminative power of embeddings inputted to Encoder. The fashion in which we expand transformers to include lexical dependency features involves minor modifications in the neural architecture leading to negligible impact on computational complexity of the model.

As the results of this research show, injecting syntax dependencies can boost Text2Gloss model performances. Namely, our syntax-aware model overcame traditional transformers in terms of BLEU, TER and ROUGE-L F1. Meanwhile, the METEOR metric was slightly worse for our model. Furthermore, we have shown that syntax information can also assist in model learning leading to a faster modelling of complex patterns.

This preliminary research constitutes a promising starting point to reach the objectives expected for the SignON Project, in which it is planned to deployed resource-hungry translation models in cloud-based computing servers.

Further work could compare the impact of other individual, or combinations of, other linguistic features such as part of speech tags which are used in other studies using syntactic tagging for NMT (Sennrich and Haddow, 2016; Armengol Estapé and Ruiz Costa-Jussà, 2021). It may also use more widely-used lexical dependency tags such as the Universal Dependencies treebank (Borges Völker et al., 2019). Moreover, we are currently exploring data augmentation techniques to expand the scarce availability of SL data.

Acknowledgements

We thank the reviewers for their comments and suggestions. This work has been conducted within the SignON project. SignON is a Horizon 2020 project, funded under the Horizon 2020 program ICT-57-2020 - "An empowering, inclusive, Next Generation Internet" with Grant Agreement number 101017255.

References

Stefanie Albert, Jan Anderssen, Regine Bader, Stephanie Becker, Tobias Bracht, Sabine Brants, Thorsten Brants, Vera Demberg, Stefanie Dipper, and Peter Eisenberg. 2003. TIGER Annotationsschema. *Universität des Saarlandes and Universität Stuttgart and Universität Potsdam*, pages 1–148.

	Example 1
Source	und nun die wettervorhersage für morgen samstag den zwölften september (EN) And now the weather forecast for tomorrow Saturday the twelfth of September
Target	JETZT WETTER MORGEN SAMSTAG ZWOELF SEPTEMBER (EN) NOW WEATHER TOMORROW SATURDAY TWELVE SEPTEMBER
	Syntax
5	JETZT WETTER WETTER (EN) NOW WEATHER WEATHER
50	JETZT WETTER WIE-AUSSEHEN MORGEN SAMSTAG FUENFTE MAI (EN) NOW WEATHER LOOK TOMORROW SATURDAY FIFTH MAY
100	JETZT WETTER WIE-AUSSEHEN MORGEN SAMSTAG ZWOELF SEPTEMBER (EN) NOW WEATHER LOOK TOMORROW SATURDAY TWELVE SEPTEMBER
150	JETZT WETTER WIE-AUSSEHEN MORGEN SAMSTAG ZWOELF SEPTEMBER (EN) NOW WEATHER LOOK TOMORROW SATURDAY TWELVE SEPTEMBER
	No-syntax
5	JETZT WETTER WIE WIE WIE-AUSSE...AUSSEAUSS (EN) NOW WEATHER HOW HOW AUSSE...AUSSEAUSS
50	JETZT WETTER WIE-AUSSEHEN MORGEN SAMSTAG FUENFZEHN SEPTEMBER (EN) NOW WEATHER LOOK TOMORROW SATURDAY FIFTEEN SEPTEMBER
100	JETZT MORGEN WETTER WIE-AUSSEHEN SAMSTAG ZWOELF SEPTEMBER (EN) NOW TOMORROW WEATHER LOOK SATURDAY TWELVE SEPTEMBER
150	JETZT MORGEN WETTER WIE-AUSSEHEN SAMSTAG ZWOELF SEPTEMBER (EN) NOW TOMORROW WEATHER LOOK SATURDAY TWELVE SEPTEMBER
	Example 2
Source	vom nordmeer zieht ein kräftiges tief heran und bringt uns ab den morgenstunden heftige schneefälle zum teil auch gefrierenden regen (EN) From the North Sea, a strong deep pulls up and brings us violent snowfalls from the morning hours, sometimes freezing rain
Target	KRAEFTIG AB MORGEN FRUEH MEISTENS SCHNEE SCHNEIEN KALT REGEN (EN) SKIMPY FROM TOMORROW EARLY MOSTLY SNOW SNOW COLD RAIN
	Syntax
5	KOMMEN REGION KOMMEN (EN) COME REGION COME
50	TIEF KOMMEN MORGEN KOMMEN REGEN KOMMEN REGEN KOMMEN (EN) DEEP COME TOMORROW COME RAIN COME RAIN COME
100	TIEF KOMMEN REGEN KOMMEN MITTE BERG KOMMEN (EN) NOW WEATHER LOOK TOMORROW SATURDAY TWELVE SEPTEMBER
150	JETZT IN-KOMMEND TIEF KOMMEN REGEN KOMMEN MILD (EN) NOW IN-COMING DEEP COME RAIN COME MILD
	No-syntax
5	REGION KOMMEN REGION KOMMEN REGEN (EN) REGION COME REGION COME RAIN
50	MORGEN KOMMEN TIEF KOMMEN REGEN KOMMEN REGEN KOMMEN REGEN KOMMEN REGEN KOMMEN (EN) TOMORROW COME DEEP COME RAIN COME RAIN COME RAIN COME RAIN COME
100	TMORGEN REGEN TIEF KOMMEN REGION KOMMEN REGEN KOENNEN SCHNEE REGEN GEFRIEREN GLATT GEFAHR GLATT GEFAHR (EN) TOMORROW RAIN DEEP COME REGION COME RAIN CAN SNOW RAIN FREEZE SMOOTH DANGER SMOOTH DANGER
150	MORGEN MEISTENS SCHNEE REGEN GLATT REGION KOMMEN REGEN GEFAHR GLATT REGEN GEFAHR GLATT REGEN GEFAHR (EN) TOMORROW MOSTLY SNOW RAIN SMOOTH REGION COME RAIN DANGER SMOOTH RAIN DANGER SMOOTH RAIN DANGER

Table 4: Some translation examples

Inês Almeida, Luísa Coheur, and Sara Candeias. 2015. From European Portuguese to Portuguese Sign Language. In *Proceedings of SLPAT 2015: 6th Workshop on Speech and Language Processing for Assistive Technologies*, pages 140–143, Dresden, Germany. Association for Computational Linguistics.

Jordi Armengol Estapé and Marta Ruiz Costa-Jussà. 2021. Semantic and syntactic information for neural machine translation: Injecting features to the transformer. *Machine Translation*, 35:3:3–17.

Satanjeev Banerjee and Alon Lavie. 2005. METEOR: An automatic metric for MT evaluation with improved correlation with human judgments. In *Proceedings of the ACL Workshop on Intrinsic and Extrinsic Evaluation Measures for Machine Translation and/or Summarization*, pages 65–72, Ann Arbor, Michigan. Association for Computational Linguistics.

Larwan Berke, Sushant Kafle, and Matt Huenerfauth. 2018. Methods for evaluation of imperfect captioning tools by deaf or hard-of-hearing users at different reading literacy levels. In *Proceedings of the 2018 CHI Conference on Human Factors in Computing Systems*, CHI '18, page 1–12, New York, NY, USA. Association for Computing Machinery.

Emanuel Borges Völker, Maximilian Wendt, Felix Hennig, and Arne Köhn. 2019. HDT-UD: A very large Universal Dependencies treebank for German. In *Proceedings of the Third Workshop on Universal Dependencies (UDW, SyntaxFest 2019)*, pages 46–57, Paris, France. Association for Computational Linguistics.

Sabine Brants, Stefanie Dipper, Peter Eisenberg, Silvia Hansen-Schirra, Esther König, Wolfgang Lezius, Christian Rohrer, George Smith, and Hans Uszkoreit. 2004. TIGER: Linguistic interpretation of a german corpus. *Journal of Language and Computation*, 2:597–620.

Carmen Cabeza, José María García-Miguel, Carmen García-Mateo, and Jose Luis Alba-Castro. 2016. Corilse: a spanish sign language repository for linguistic analysis. In *of the Language Resources and Evaluation Conference, Portorož (Slovenia)*, pages 23–28.

Necati Camgoz, Simon Hadfield, Oscar Koller, Hermann Ney, and Richard Bowden. 2018. Neural sign language translation. In *2018 IEEE/CVF Conference on Computer Vision and Pattern Recognition*, pages 7784–7793.

Necati Cihan Camgoz, Oscar Koller, Simon Hadfield, and Richard Bowden. 2020. Sign language transformers: Joint end-to-end sign language recognition and translation. In *2020 IEEE/CVF Conference on Computer Vision and Pattern Recognition (CVPR)*, pages 10020–10030.

Jacob Devlin, Ming-Wei Chang, Kenton Lee, and Kristina Toutanova. 2019. BERT: Pre-training of deep bidirectional transformers for language understanding. In *Proceedings of the 2019 Conference of the North American Chapter of the Association for Computational Linguistics: Human Language Technologies, Volume 1 (Long and Short Papers)*, pages 4171–4186, Minneapolis, Minnesota. Association for Computational Linguistics.

David M. Eberhard, Gary F. Simons, and Charles D. Fennig. 2021. *Ethnologue: Languages of the World*, twenty-fourth edition. SIL International, Dallas, TX, USA.

Thomas Hanke. 2004. Hamnosys—representing sign language data in language resources and language processing contexts. In *LREC 2004, Workshop proceedings: Representation and processing of sign languages*, pages 1–6, Paris, France.

Hany Hassan, Anthony Aue, C. Chen, Vishal Chowdhary, J. Clark, C. Federmann, Xuedong Huang, Marcin Junczys-Dowmunt, W. Lewis, M. Li, Shujie Liu, T. Liu, Renqian Luo, Arul Menezes, Tao Qin, F. Seide, Xu Tan, Fei Tian, Lijun Wu, Shuangzhi Wu, Yingce Xia, Dongdong Zhang, Zhirui Zhang, and M. Zhou. 2018. Achieving human parity on automatic chinese to english news translation. *ArXiv*, abs/1803.05567:1–25.

Tommi Jantunen, Rebekah Rousi, Päivi Raino, Markku Turunen, Mohammad Valipoor, and Narciso García. 2021. *Is There Any Hope for Developing Automated Translation Technology for Sign Languages?*, pages 61–73.

Melvin Johnson, Mike Schuster, Quoc V. Le, Maxim Krikun, Yonghui Wu, Zhifeng Chen, Nikhil Thorat, Fernanda Viégas, Martin Wattenberg, Greg Corrado, Macduff Hughes, and Jeffrey Dean. 2017. Google's multilingual neural machine translation system: Enabling zero-shot translation. *Transactions of the Association for Computational Linguistics*, 5:339–351.

Philipp Koehn. 2009. *Statistical Machine Translation*. Cambridge University Press.

Taku Kudo and John Richardson. 2018. SentencePiece: A simple and language independent subword tokenizer and detokenizer for neural text processing. In *Proceedings of the 2018 Conference on Empirical Methods in Natural Language Processing: System Demonstrations*, pages 66–71, Brussels, Belgium. Association for Computational Linguistics.

Mike Lewis, Yinhan Liu, Naman Goyal, Marjan Ghazvininejad, Abdelrahman Mohamed, Omer Levy, Veselin Stoyanov, and Luke Zettlemoyer. 2020. BART: Denoising sequence-to-sequence pre-training for natural language generation, translation, and comprehension. In *Proceedings of the 58th Annual Meeting of the Association for Computational Linguistics*, pages 7871–7880, Online. Association for Computational Linguistics.

Chin-Yew Lin. 2004. ROUGE: A package for automatic evaluation of summaries. In *Text Summarization Branches Out*, pages 74–81, Barcelona, Spain. Association for Computational Linguistics.

Yinhan Liu, Jiatao Gu, Naman Goyal, Xian Li, Sergey Edunov, Marjan Ghazvininejad, Mike Lewis, and Luke Zettlemoyer. 2020. Multilingual denoising pre-training for neural machine translation. *CoRR*, abs/2001.08210:1–17.

V. López-Ludeña, C. González-Morcillo, J.C. López, R. Barra-Chicote, R. Cordoba, and R. San-Segundo. 2014. Translating bus information into sign language for deaf people. *Engineering Applications of Artificial Intelligence*, 32:258–269.

Amit Moryossef, Kayo Yin, Graham Neubig, and Yoav Goldberg. 2021. Data augmentation for sign language gloss translation. *CoRR*, abs/2105.07476:1–7.

Medet Mukushev, Arman Sabyrov, Alfarabi Imashev, Kenessary Koishybay, Vadim Kimmelman, and

Anara Sandygulova. 2020. Evaluation of manual and non-manual components for sign language recognition. In *Proceedings of the 12th Language Resources and Evaluation Conference*, pages 6073–6078, Marseille, France. European Language Resources Association.

Fabrizio Nunnari, Cristina España-Bonet, and Eleftherios Avramidis. 2021. A data augmentation approach for sign-language-to-text translation in-the-wild. In *Proceedings of the 3rd Conference on Language, Data and Knowledge. Conference on Language, Data and Knowledge (LDK-2020), September 1-3, Zaragoza, Spain, Spain*, volume 93 of *OpenAccess Series in Informatics (OASIcs)*. Dagstuhl publishing.

Kishore Papineni, Salim Roukos, Todd Ward, and Wei-Jing Zhu. 2002. Bleu: a method for automatic evaluation of machine translation. In *Proceedings of the 40th Annual Meeting of the Association for Computational Linguistics*, pages 311–318, Philadelphia, Pennsylvania, USA. Association for Computational Linguistics.

Jordi Porta, Fernando López-Colino, Javier Tejedor, and José Colás. 2014. A rule-based translation from written spanish to spanish sign language glosses. *Computer Speech & Language*, 28:788–811.

Matt Post. 2018. A call for clarity in reporting BLEU scores. In *Proceedings of the Third Conference on Machine Translation: Research Papers*, pages 186–191, Belgium, Brussels. Association for Computational Linguistics.

H. Saggion, D. Shterionov, G. Labaka, T. Van de Cruys, V. Vandeghinste, and J. Blat. 2021. SignON: Bridging the gap between Sign and Spoken Languages. In *Proceedings of the 37th Conference of the Spanish Society for Natural Language Processing*, Málaga, Spain (held on-line). SEPLN.

Rubén San-Segundo, Verónica López, Raquel Martín, David Sánchez, and Adolfo García. 2010. Language resources for spanish - spanish sign language (lse) translation. In *Proceedings of the 4th Workshop on the Representation and Processing of Sign Languages: Corpora and Sign Languages Technologies*, pages 208–211.

Rico Sennrich and Barry Haddow. 2016. Linguistic input features improve neural machine translation. In *Proceedings of the First Conference on Machine Translation: Volume 1, Research Papers*, pages 83–91, Berlin, Germany. Association for Computational Linguistics.

Matthew Snover, Bonnie Dorr, Rich Schwartz, Linnea Micciulla, and John Makhoul. 2006. A study of translation edit rate with targeted human annotation. pages 223–231.

Richard Socher, John Bauer, Christopher D. Manning, and Andrew Y. Ng. 2013. Parsing with compositional vector grammars. In *Proceedings of the 51st Annual Meeting of the Association for Computational Linguistics (Volume 1: Long Papers)*, pages 455–465, Sofia, Bulgaria. Association for Computational Linguistics.

Stephanie Stoll, Necati Cihan Camgöz, Simon Hadfield, and Richard Bowden. 2020. Text2sign: Towards sign language production using neural machine translation and generative adversarial networks. *Int. J. Comput. Vis.*, 128(4):891–908.

Ashish Vaswani, Noam Shazeer, Niki Parmar, Jakob Uszkoreit, Llion Jones, Aidan N. Gomez, Lukasz Kaiser, and Illia Polosukhin. 2017. Attention is all you need. In *Proceedings of the 31st International Conference on Neural Information Processing Systems*, NIPS'17, page 6000–6010.

Linting Xue, Noah Constant, Adam Roberts, Mihir Kale, Rami Al-Rfou, Aditya Siddhant, Aditya Barua, and Colin Raffel. 2021. mT5: A massively multilingual pre-trained text-to-text transformer. In *Proceedings of the 2021 Conference of the North American Chapter of the Association for Computational Linguistics: Human Language Technologies*, pages 483–498, Online. Association for Computational Linguistics.

Kayo Yin and Jesse Read. 2020. Better sign language translation with STMC-transformer. In *Proceedings of the 28th International Conference on Computational Linguistics*, pages 5975–5989, Barcelona, Spain (Online). International Committee on Computational Linguistics.

I. Zwitserlood, M. Verlinden, J. Ros, and Sanny van der Schoot. 2004. Synthetic signing for the deaf : eSIGN.

Employing Wikipedia as a Resource for Named Entity Recognition in Morphologically Complex Under-Resourced Languages

Aravind Krishnan[1,3], Stefan Ziehe[2], Franziska Pannach[3], and Caroline Sporleder[2,3]

aravindhp1999@gmail.com,
{caroline.sporleder,stefan.ziehe}@cs.uni-goettingen.de,
franziska.pannach@uni-goettingen.de

[1]College of Engineering Trivandrum, India
[2]Institute of Computer Science, University of Göttingen, Germany
[3]Göttingen Centre for Digital Humanities, Germany

Abstract

We propose a novel approach for rapid prototyping of named entity recognisers through the development of semi-automatically annotated data sets. We demonstrate the proposed pipeline on two under-resourced agglutinating languages: the Dravidian language *Malayalam* and the Bantu language *isiZulu*. Our approach is weakly supervised and bootstraps training data from Wikipedia and Google Knowledge Graph. Moreover, our approach is relatively language independent and can consequently be ported quickly (and hence cost-effectively) from one language to another, requiring only minor language-specific tailoring.

1 Introduction

Named entity recognition (NER) is the task of identifying proper names and assigning them to one of several named entity (NE) classes, such as PERSON (PER), LOCATION (LOC) or ORGANISATION (ORG), which is a crucial processing step for many NLP tasks, but also for many applications in the digital humanities where information about the entities involved (e.g. names of emperors or archaelogical sites) is often particularly important. While state-of-the-art systems obtain good results for standard NE inventories and general purpose English (Chiu and Nichols, 2016), annotated data sets for the development of named entity taggers are not readily available for most of the world's languages.[1]

In this paper, we focus on semi-automatically generating annotated data and bootstrapping NE recognisers for under-resourced languages (cf. Krauwer (2003)), i.e., languages for which manually annotated data as well as pre-processing tools, such as part-of-speech taggers, are typically hard to come by. To this end, we propose a *weakly supervised* approach that bootstraps the training set from Wikipedia (in the target language) and Google knowledge graph (in English), requiring no manual annotation and no pre-processing apart from the language-specific tweaking of our matching heuristics. This approach is therefore in principle suitable for any language for which Wikipedia articles exist.[2] Because the manual effort is limited, systems can be quickly ported to new languages, while still obtaining reasonable results.

We demonstrate this by developing the system for *Malayalam* and then porting it to *isiZulu*. These two languages were chosen because they are agglutinating and morphologically complex, making the task considerably more challenging than for many Indo-European languages where NEs are only minimally inflected. While our target languages are both agglutinating, they are also structurally quite different in other respects and exhibit different degrees of "under-resourcing", with noticeably fewer resources being available for isiZulu (see Sect. 3)

2 Related Work

Wikipedia has been employed for NER in three main ways: In a monolingual setting, early studies used it to extract Gazetteer lists which were then used as features in (typically supervised) NER systems. One of the first studies taking this approach was by Toral and Muñoz (2006), who extract Gazetteers by matching the first sentence of a Wikipedia article heuristically against the WordNet

[1]Even for English, NER is not necessarily a solved problem for specialised domains, which often require specific entity class inventories (Brandsen et al., 2020).

[2]As of July 2021 this applies to 323 languages. Arguably this still leaves out a large amount of the world's 6000+ languages but it covers many languages which have a fair amount of speakers but are still under-resourced. Furthermore, Wikipedia is constantly growing both in terms of content for a given language and in terms of the languages it covers.

Proceedings of 14th Workshop on Building and Using Comparable Corpora in conjunction with RANLP-2021, pages 28–39, held online, 6 September 2021.
https://doi.org/10.26615/978-954-452-076-2_005

(Fellbaum, 1998) noun hierarchy to identify the category of the entity described. This was followed by a number of similar approaches (Kazama and Torisawa, 2007; Ratinov and Roth, 2009; Radford et al., 2015).

Going one step further, some researchers used Wikipedia not only for extracting Gazetteers but also for bootstrapping annotated training data. For example, Nothman et al. (2008) exploit hyperlinks to annotate the sentences containing them with category information, which is extracted from the article the hyperlink links *to*. As not all mentions of an entity in an article are hyperlinked, they extend the data set by finding verbatim repetitions of the hyperlink's anchor text in the article. Finally, they use the data to train an NE tagger. The system requires hand-labelling of seed data that maps information extracted from articles to NE classes.

Wikipedia has also been used in a multilingual setting to obtain NE taggers for languages other than English, e.g. by exploiting cross-lingual links between articles (Richman and Schone, 2008; Bhagavatula et al., 2012; Pan et al., 2017). This approach has also been applied to under-resourced languages (Littell et al., 2016). Ni and Florian (2016) go one step further and construct entity type mappings for the English Wikipedia before projecting across Wikipedia language links.

Bouamor et al. (Bouamor et al., 2013) propose employing Wikipedia as a resource for creating domain-specific lexicons for machine-translation. They demonstrate their approach for English-French and English-Romanian translation tasks. Mayhew et al. (Mayhew et al., 2017) combine lexicon-based translation of training data from a source to a target language with features generated from Wikipedia and show that this approach can be applied to under-resourced languages.

Studies that address NER for our target languages are very limited. To our knowledge the first NER system for Malayalam was proposed by Bindu and Idicula (2011), who use supervised machine learning utilising a variety of features complemented with a finite-state automaton to deal with complex words. Jayan et al. (2013) propose a hybrid approach that combines rules with supervised machine learning. Devi et al. (2016) tackle named entity extraction from social media and combine supervised machine learning (SVMs) with skip-gram features. Shruthi and Pranav (2016) propose another supervised approach based on the TnT tagger (Brants, 2002) and maximum entropy models. A neural network approach is proposed by Ajees and Idicula (2018) who use word embeddings of context words and morphs of the target word as features. A similar system but with a different neural architecture (RNN-LSTM) has also been proposed (Sreeja and Pillai, 2020). To our knowledge, the only NER system for isiZulu was proposed by Eiselen (2016), who used linear-chain Conditional Random Fields (CRFs) for the classification of the named entities. The features included gazetteer lists and graphemic information (capitalization, punctuation, numerals).

3 The Target Languages: Malayalam and isiZulu

We test our system on two agglutinating languages: Malayalam and isiZulu. We hypothesise that inflection and agglutination will make the task particularly challenging, as one token can correspond to several linguistic words (see Sec. 3.1 and 3.2). However, Malayalam and isiZulu also differ in several aspects: They use different writing systems (Brahmic vs. Latin) and while the former tends to make extensive use of suffixes the latter tends to favour prefixes to encode grammatical information. From a practical perspective, while both languages are under-resourced, isiZulu is so to a greater extent, in particular its Wikipedia version is more than an order of magnitude smaller (see Sec. 4). We thus believe that these two languages pose sufficiently heterogeneous use cases.

3.1 Malayalam

Malayalam is the official language of the Indian state of Kerala. It is a Dravidian language and shares its roots with other south Indian languages such as Tamil and Telegu. Malayalam is spoken by 45 million people, mainly in Kerala, Lakshadeep and Puducherry. Like most Dravidian languages, Malayalam has a Subject-Object-Verb canonical order. It is a heavily agglutinating language. Finite verbs in Malayalam are inflected based on tense and mood, and are invariant to gender or number. Inflection is usually carried out through suffixing. A noun in Malayalam can be suffixed in at least 7 different ways according to the case and grammatical category employed.

For example, “Kochi” (കൊച്ചി) is a place in Kerala. കൊച്ചി*യിൽ* means “*inside/in Kochi*”. കൊച്ചി*യിൽനിന്നും* means *from Kochi* and കൊച്ചി*യുടെ* means *of Kochi*. The word can be be inflected in various other ways as well. An example of suffixing within a sentence is depicted in (1).

(1) ഹനുമാൻ സീത + യെ കാണുവാൻ
Hanuman Seetha + accusative to see
ലങ്ക + യിലേക്ക് പോയി
Lanka + to go
‘Hanuman went to Lanka to see Seetha’

Agglutination is optional in Malayalam. Therefore, a word has the option of merging with another consecutive word, producing a new word in the process. For example, കൊച്ചിയിൽ ആയിരുന്നു (കൊച്ചിയിൽ: in Kochi, ആയിരുന്നു: was) translates to *was in Kochi*. The two words can be optionally combined into a new token: കൊച്ചിയിലായിരുന്നു (*was in Kochi*). Grammatically speaking, the split version and the agglutinated version can be used interchangeably in a sentence. This increases the complexity of token matching and dictionary generation significantly. Furthermore, unlike languages written in Latin script, Malayalam does not distinguish between upper and lower case in its writing system, hence casing cannot be used as a cue for named entity recognition.

Although it is an under-resourced language, the presence of Malayalam in the form of articles and data repositories on the internet has been growing steadily over the years. It has featured in a limited number of NLP tasks, including morphological analysis (Bhavukam et al., 2018), POS tagging (Akhil et al., 2020) and NER (Ajees and Idicula, 2018). However, many studies use small locally generated data sets (Nambiar et al., 2019) or domain specific data sets (Kumar et al., 2019), (Devi et al., 2016), which usually are not freely available.

3.2 IsiZulu

IsiZulu is the language of the Zulu people in Southern Africa. It is spoken by approximately 10.6 Million people (Taljard and Bosch, 2006), mainly in the eastern part of South Africa and Mozambique. IsiZulu is an agglutinating, conjunctively-written language and belongs to the Bantu languages (Nguni sub-branch) (Taljard and Bosch, 2006). As is characteristic for Bantu languages, isiZulu uses noun classes, e.g. dedicated classes for nouns describing humans in singular or plural.

Certain natural language processing tasks can be very challenging or almost infeasible to solve for languages such as isiZulu. For instance, due to the nature of isiZulu concords, prefixes and infixes[3], sentences might consist of ambiguous words, as in Example (2). Another characteristic that isiZulu shares with other conjunctive languages is the use of capitalization inside a word, which can be an indicator of a named entity, e.g. *eGoli* – in/from Johannesburg, as in (3). Cultural naming conventions are another challenge for NER (Eiselen, 2016). For example, *Nkosi* means *king, lord* or *chief* and can be both first- or lastname, as for the South African rugby players S’busiso Nkosi and Nkosi Nofuma.

(2) Aba+ fundi a+
CLASS-2-NOUN-PREFIX-PL. learn NEG
ba+ fund+ i.
SUBJ-CONDORD learn NEG
‘The students are not learning.’

(3) Umfo+ wethu u+
brother 1ST-PERS-POSS SUBJ.-CONCORD
hlala e+ Goli.
stay LOC Johannesburg
‘My brother stays in Johannesburg.’

While isiZulu is not an endangered language[4], there is a lack of large digital textual resources, such as newspaper archives, and consequently also of NLP tools. The South African Centre for Digital Language Resources (SADiLaR) is one of the main drivers of language development in South Africa. Besides their teaching and knowledge sharing efforts, SADiLaR also collects resources for the South African languages and makes them available through their website[5]. The SADiLaR repository currenty lists 49 language resources, tools and corpora for isiZulu.

4 Data Sets and Resources

For bootstrapping **training** data, we utilise the **Malayalam** and **isiZulu Wikipedias**. The former is significantly larger (65,000 vs. 2,701 articles as of June 2020) and therefore also gives rise to a larger training set. In order to find appropriate named entity tags for Wikipedia articles (see Sect. 5.2) we employ the **Google Knowledge Graph**

[3] https://en.wiktionary.org/wiki/Category:Zulu_prefixes

[4] https://glottolog.org/resource/languoid/id/zulu1248

[5] https://www.sadilar.org/index.php/en/

(GKG) (Singhal, 2012). We **test** our system on two external data sets for Malayalam (ARNEKT and CUSAT) and one for isiZulu (NCHLT II) as well as part of our bootstrapped data:

ARNEKT IECSIL FIRE 2018 NER Dataset This corpus was compiled from the abstracts and info-box properties from DBpedia for the (IECSIL) shared task (Hullathy Balakrishnan et al., 2018). The info-box features are used to annotate long abstracts. Meta tags are translated into English using Google translator. The data set consists of 838,333 tokens overall: 59,422 PER, 29,371 LOC, and 4,841 ORG. All other tokens are labelled OTHER.

CUSAT NER Dataset This is a manually annotated NER data set developed by CUSAT.[6] It is based on the CUSAT POS tagged data set for Malayalam (Ajees and Idicula, 2018). About 200,000 words from "internet texts" were manually annotated. The POS tags were ignored and the data was cleaned to remove special characters. The data set consists of 190,265 tokens overall, with 1,864 PER, 1,035 LOC, and 496 ORG entities. It is thus considerably smaller than the ARNEKT data set.

NCHLT II Dataset This isiZulu data set consists of South African governmental texts, which are manually annotated with named entities (Eiselen, 2016), containing 5,024 PER, 3,872 LOC, and 5,039 ORG, 1,8224 MISC (i.e. other entity classes), and 169,393 OUT (non-entities) tokens. For evaluation, we merge the latter two classes to OTHER.

WikiML and WikiZu Apart from ARNEKT, the above data sets come from other domains as our training data (Wikipedia). Hence, testing on them can be seen as an out-of-domain lower bound evaluation of our system. For comparison, we therefore also test on a 10% portion of our Wikipedia data sets (see Sect. 5). This constitutes an upper bound as these data sets are from the same domain as the training data but are labelled automatically in a fashion identical to labelling the training data, which might lead to overly optimistic results.

5 Bootstrapping the Training Data

As our focus is on under-resourced languages, we do not assume that a manually labelled training set is available. Instead we bootstrap from Wikipedia and GKG. Utilising Wikipedia has a number of advantages: First, as it is community-driven, many under-resourced languages have a version of Wikipedia. Second, Wikipedia articles cover a wide range of subjects and often refer to named entities. Third, Wikipedia has a number of features that help with bootstrapping entity labels (see Sect. 2). Finally, it has been shown that additional training data bootstrapped from Wikipedia can also improve the performance of taggers trained on other sources, especially if they are applied out-of-domain (Nothman et al., 2009).

We employ a 4-step pipeline to bootstrap NE labelled data (Fig. 1): First, we extract a list of titles from Wikipedia dumps in the target language. Second, we use the Wikipedia language links to look up their English counterparts. Third, we employ the GKG to extract candidates for named entity tags. Finally, we use the title list to annotate Wikipedia articles. The distribution of the different NE tags for both data sets is shown in Table 1.

NE Tag	Malayalam	isiZulu
Other	21012137	138986
Place	723259	5916
Person	444260	2748
Organization	179022	700
Total	**22358678**	**148350**

Table 1: NE token distribution, compiled data sets

5.1 Creation of the Title Lists

We compile a list of all article titles from the Wikipedia dump of the target language[7] and preprocess it by removing all entries that do not contain at least one character in the target language. This removes titles entirely composed of numbers, special characters and characters from other languages. Duplicate titles are also removed. The title list includes titles which share the primary token, but contain descriptors in brackets to distinguish them, for example ഉണ്ണിയാർച്ച: *Unniyarcha* and ഉണ്ണിയാർച്ച (ചലച്ചിത്രം): *Unniyarcha (Film)*, where the descriptor helps distinguish the person from the movie. Descriptors are preserved, because they are vital when annotating the title with an NE tag.

[6] https://www.cusat.ac.in/

[7] For Malayalam, we used a Wikipedia dump from July 2020, for isiZulu from January 2021.

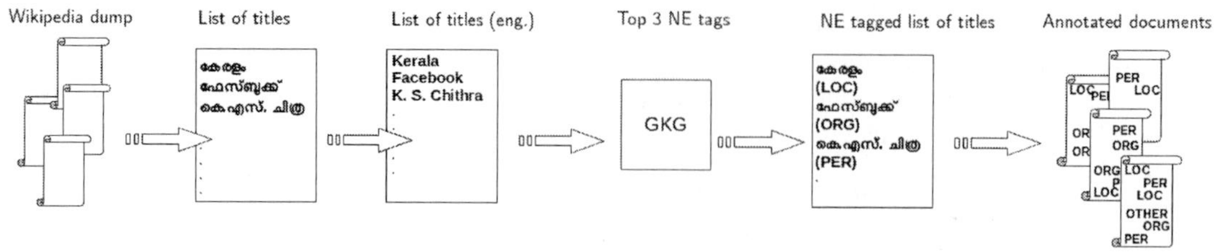

Figure 1: Schematic overview of the data set generation process

5.2 Labeling Titles with NE Tags

In order to assign titles their respective NE tags, we query each title in the title list through the GKG, which associates the search result with a tag similar to entity tags used in NER systems. For the purpose of this study, the tags have been limited to PER, LOC and ORG, since they are the most widely employed entity types. Entities that do not fall into these categories are labelled OTHER. As the GKG accepts only English queries, we need to translate (and transliterate for Malayalam) titles from the target languages. We exploit the multilingualism in Wikipedia to map titles from the target language to their respective counterparts in English.

The GKG makes use of different sources when producing tags and will generate a ranked list of (possibly different) tags for each query. We consider only the top three of these. If one of the three named entity tags appears in this list, it is assigned to the respective title, with priority being given to the higher ranking source. If the tags generated by the GKG do not contain any of our named entities, the title is annotated with the tag OTHER (i.e. no named entity or a named entity belonging to a different category such as DATE). We then automatically annotate the text of each Wikipedia article, assigning each token one of three NE tags (PERS, LOC, ORG) or the tag OTHER. As illustrated in Figure 2, we perform two "sweeps":

The first stage of the first sweep exploits hyperlinks to annotate tokens within an article. Even if a title present in the body of the article is ambiguous, a hyperlink will direct to the correct source and tag. For example, tokens that have different NE tags but the same primary token, e.g. *Unniyarcha* and *Unniyarcha (Film)*, can be disambiguated by extracting the corresponding named entity tag for each hyperlink from the title list created earlier. Then, the descriptions within brackets are removed in the case of ambiguous titles. All appearances of hyperlinks are annotated with their respective tags. Tokens that do not match any hyperlink are labelled OTHER.

In the second stage of the first sweep, all occurrences of titles that are not hyperlinked in the article body are annotated. For each article, the tokens labelled OTHER after the first stage are compared with the named entity titles in the title list. All token matches are annotated with the tag of the respective title.

In the second sweep, we annotate tokens that match sub-words of named entity titles in our title list, i.e., we annotate inflected forms and complex words. This is necessary because, in agglutinating languages, proper nouns seldom exist in their base form. This makes the matching of words that refer to the same concept harder than for languages such as English, which only has minimal pre- and suffixing, because a simple search for string equality with a title will not suffice. Therefore, we developed language-specific token-title matching algorithms discussed in the next sections. Since the secondary sweep is executed only after the ambiguous tokens are dealt with, the annotation procedure tackles both reliability and quantity of annotations.

5.3 Accommodating Morphological Characteristics

5.3.1 Heuristics for Malayalam

Suffix matching A major problem for NER in Malayalam is that —due to inflection and agglutination— nouns rarely occur in their base form but are typically adorned by suffixes. To solve this problem, a suffix stripping algorithm is employed, which initially compares each title in the list with the tokens in the body of the article and extracts all tokens that qualify a basic distance match. A threshold of 70% match was empirically found to work well. To counteract overgeneration and ensure the presence of suffixation, the results are

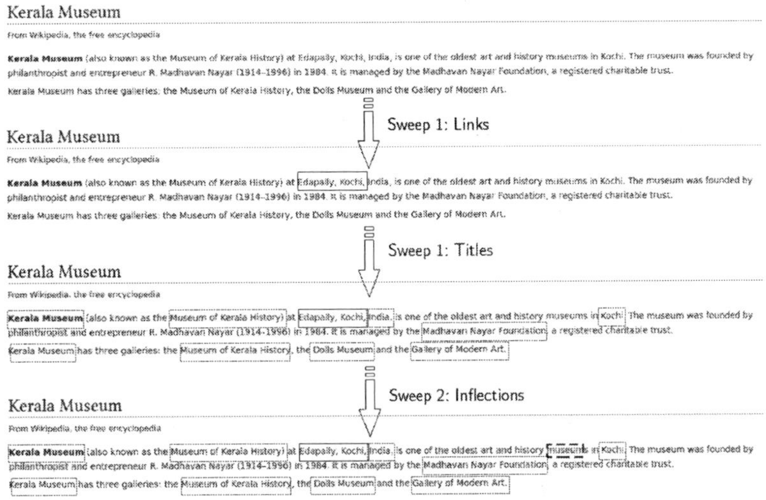

Figure 2: Overview of the three stages of data set annotation

further filtered by checking if the token begins with the root word. That is, the first $(n-1)$ characters of the token must match the first $(n-1)$ characters of the title, for a title of length n. This separates suffixed versions from accidental matches. For example, the title പന്തളം (Panthalam-*Place*) matches both പന്തയം (Panthayam-*competition*) and പന്തളവും (Panthala+vum-*Panthalam as well*). Only the second token is an inflected version. The suffix match with the first $(n-1)$ characters ('പ', 'ന്ത', 'ള') extracts the inflected token and discards arbitrary matches.

Attachment of the place of origin to a person's name It is a common practice in Kerala to attach the place of a person's origin to their name. For example, consider the name Pinarayi Vijayan (പിണറായി വിജയൻ). The individual's name is "Vijayan" (വിജയൻ), while "Pinarayi" (പിണറായി) is the place where he is from. The title list would consist of both "പിണറായി-Place" and "പിണറായി വിജയൻ- Person". When a bigram check is employed first, all instances of "പിണറായി വിജയൻ" are annotated with the tag "Person". The tokens in the article body are annotated "പിണറായി- Person, വിജയൻ- Person". If this is followed by the annotation of "പിണറായി", the token "പിണറായി വിജയൻ" is modified to " പിണറായി- Place, വിജയൻ-Person". To avoid this behaviour for Malayalam, uni-grams are always annotated first and then followed by higher order n grams.

Punctuation in names Another common practice is the usage of acronyms within the name. For example, *Madath Thekkepaattu Vasudevan Nair* usually goes by *M.T. Vasudevan Nair* (എം.ടി. വാസുദേവൻ നായർ). The name is sometimes tokenized as ("എം.", "ടി.", "വാസുദേവൻ", "നായർ") or as ("എം" ,"." , "ടി.", "വാസുദേവൻ", "നായർ"). In some other cases, the article omits the punctuation, and prints the name as ("എം", "ടി", "വാസുദേവൻ", "നായർ"). Since the number of tokens within the title changes, the n-gram search consequently varies. Since this issue is specific to full stops ("."), all full stops are removed from both the article and the titles during the search phase. After all appearances of the individual tokens sans punctuation are annotated within the article, the full stops are reinserted. If the tokens to either side of the full stop have the same NE tag, the full stop is given the same tag as the tokens that wrap around it. All end-of-sentence full stops are annotated with the tag OTHER.

5.4 Language-Specific Adaptation for isiZulu

As isiZulu focuses on prefixes rather than suffixes, we perform prefix stripping for isiZulu. To this end, we make use of the capitalization described in Section 3.2. Where we could not find a full match between a title and a word in the list, we matched titles and occurrences in the text from the first capital after the initial letter. Thus, we were able to match *iGoli* and *eGoli*, i.e. Johannesburg

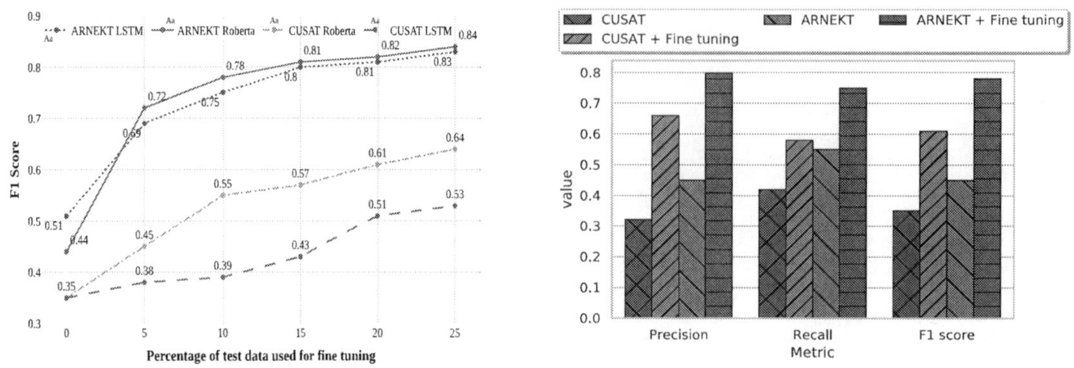

(a) Variation of F1 score with the amount of test data used for fine tuning

(b) Variation in model performance after fine tuning

Figure 3: Fine tuning analysis

→ from/in Johannesburg.

6 Experiments and Machine Learning Setup

For comparison, we use two baseline systems. One rule-based baseline annotation system and a neural network baseline. The rule-based baseline directly annotates the data sets with the title list generated in section 5.1. A bi-gram search is used to annotate titles that have two words. This procedure does not account for inflections and annotates perfect matches in the corpus. The rule-based baseline is therefore language independent. This system is used to evaluate the importance of accommodating inflection and agglutination when compiling an NER data set for morphologically complex languages.

The deep learning baseline for NER is implemented using Keras (Chollet, 2015). It is a recurrent LSTM network with the following layers:

1. Trainable linear embeddings of size 200
2. Bidirectional LSTM with 45 units for each direction; recurrent dropout probability of 0.1
3. Linear layer with 50 units and ReLU activation, applied to each time step
4. CRF layer with four units (one per NE class)

The model is trained using the RMSprop optimizer with a learning rate of 0.001 for 10 epochs.

We use XLM-RoBERTa (Conneau et al., 2019) to build the NER system. It is a pre-trained multilingual transformer model which has successfully been applied to low resourced languages such as Swahili and Urdu. The model is trained in the `xlm-roberta-base` configuration using decoupled weight decay (Loshchilov and Hutter, 2019) and layer-wise decaying learning rates (Sun et al., 2019). The embedding layer is frozen to avoid overfitting. We train the model on a TPU in Google Colab[8] using `bfloat16` mixed precision training and the following hyperparameters:

- Sequence length: 50
- Batch size: 1024
- Epochs: 10
- Base learning rate: $2 \cdot 10^{-5}$
- Weight decay factor: 0.99
- Learning rate decay factor: 0.95

The data sets are split into training, testing and validation sets by a 80:10:10 ratio.

6.1 Fine Tuning

Before testing the model with a target data set, the model is fine tuned for adaptation. A small subset of each test set is used to tune the weights and the remaining data is used to test the model. Fine tuning is carried out for two reasons: (i) to accommodate for changes in writing style and format and (ii) to expose the model to previously unseen tokens. Since agglutination and heavy inflection exists in both languages, it is practically infeasible to construct dictionaries that account for all words

[8]https://colab.research.google.com/

Table 2: XLM-RoBERTa results for Malayalam

	WikiMl			CUSAT			ARNEKT		
Class	Precision	Recall	F1 Score	Precision	Recall	F1 Score	Precision	Recall	F1 Score
Person	0.94	0.80	0.87	0.65	0.48	0.56	0.74	0.65	0.69
Place	0.93	0.83	0.87	0.55	0.57	0.56	0.76	0.78	0.77
Organization	0.79	0.82	0.81	0.48	0.28	0.35	0.75	0.62	0.68
Other	0.99	1.00	0.99	0.99	0.99	0.99	0.96	0.97	0.97
Macro Average	**0.94**	**0.80**	**0.87**	**0.66**	**0.58**	**0.61**	**0.80**	**0.75**	**0.78**

Table 3: XLM-RoBERTa results for isiZulu

	WikiZu			NCHLT II		
Class	Precision	Recall	F1 Score	Precision	Recall	F1 Score
Place	0.94	0.87	0.90	0.46	0.41	0.43
Person	0.78	0.90	0.84	0.31	0.20	0.24
Organization	0.78	0.75	0.77	0.25	0.15	0.19
Other	0.99	0.99	0.99	0.95	0.97	0.96
Macro Average	**0.9**	**0.88**	**0.89**	**0.69**	**0.56**	**0.63**

in them. During the training phase, a dictionary is created using the developed data set which is then used to feed tokens into an embedding layer. In the case of an external data set, the model encounters many words foreign to its dictionary. Fine tuning helps it to learn the appearance patterns of unknown tokens within the article.

6.2 Results for Malayalam

Figure 3a depicts the model performance when varying amounts of test data are used for fine tuning. For the ARNEKT data, tuning the model with a small portion of the test data set increases the performance drastically. Since this data set is large, even a small portion of it helps the model adapt easily. On the other hand, the smaller CUSAT data set attains a noticeable increase in model performance at a slightly higher level of fine tuning. Since fine tuning requires a sufficient amount of tokens, a slightly bigger chunk of the CUSAT data set has to be used to fine-tune the model's parameters. The effect of fine tuning on the overall performance is visualised in Figure 3b (with 10% data for ARNEKT and 20% for CUSAT). The model performance increases considerably after fine tuning, in both cases. The class-wise performance for the WikiML, ARNEKT and CUSAT data sets is shown in Table 2. As expected, the (upper bound) results for WikiML are high across all NE classes. For the ARNEKT data set, the model performs also quite well with an average F1 score of 0.78. In comparison, the out-of-domain evaluation on the CUSAT data obtains an F1 score of 0.61, with particularly low results for *org* entities. This may be due to the fact that organisations are distributed differently in this domain.

The baseline annotation system was also evaluated on the CUSAT data set and the ARNEKT data set, obtaining F1-scores of 0.29 and 0.39, respectively. This performance highlights the importance of considering inflections, and fine tuning the model for domain adaptation.

6.3 Results for isiZulu

Table 3 shows the results of porting our system to isiZulu (with 20% of the data for fine-tuning). With an average F1-Score of 0.87 our system performs well on the in-domain WikiZu data but worse in the out-of-domain evaluation on NHCLT II, with an average F1-Score of 0.45. It still easily outperforms the rule-based baseline system (0.24 F1-Score) and the LSTM baseline (0.45 F1-Score). The lower performance compared to Malayalam can be explained by the fact that the domain of the test set is very different from that of the training set (legal vs. Wikipedia) and, moreover, the training set for isiZulu is considerably smaller than for Malayalam. In this context and given that we only used 2 days to tweak the system for isiZulu, we still consider the results an encouraging first step.

7 Analysis of Results

Since testing on WikiML can be regarded as in-domain, we focus on the analysis of errors on the

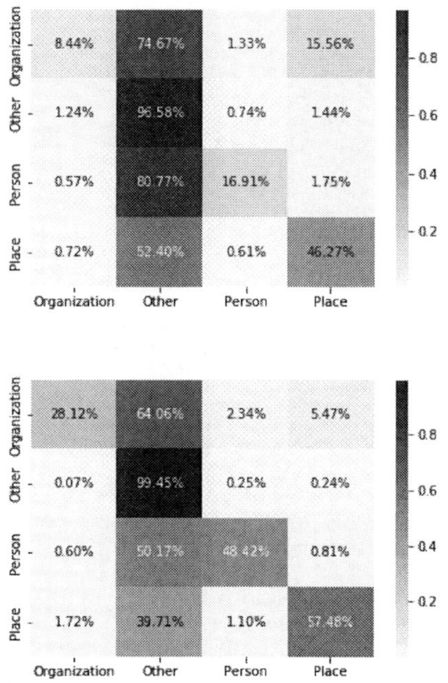

Figure 4: Confusion Matrix for CUSAT before (above) and after (below) fine tuning

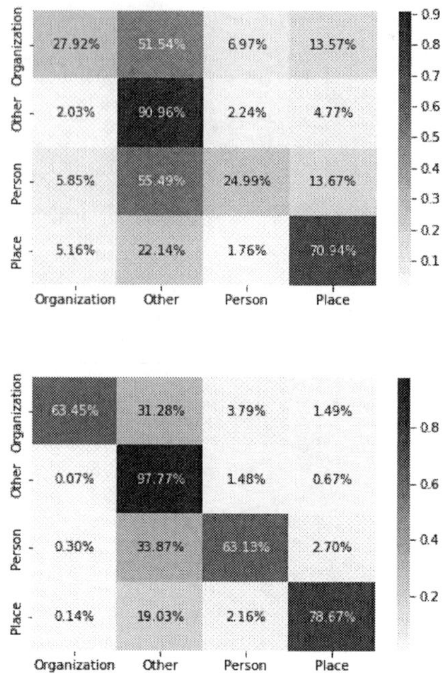

Figure 5: Confusion Matrix for ARNEKT before (above) and after (below) fine tuning

external data sets. Figures 4 and 5 display the confusion matrices of the results obtained when testing our model before and after fine tuning. In both cases, the biggest source of error is observed to be misclassification into the "Other" category. This is expected in languages with morphological complexities, since named entities are concealed within agglutinations and suffixes. It should be noted that for ARNEKT, the performance errors do not necessarily originate from the model. To our knowledge, ARNEKT was not manually annotated, but created with rule based annotation procedures and word lists. Consequently, annotation errors can be observed within the data set. In some cases, the WikiML model is seen to predict correct named entity tags for tokens wrongly annotated in ARNEKT. Two examples are presented in (4) and (5). Wrong annotations have been highlighted in red. Fine tuning clearly improves the impact of errors involving the "Other" category significantly.

(4)

Tokens:	ഡച്ച്	സാമ്പത്തിക
ARNEKT:	**Place**	**Other**
Prediction:	Organization	Other

ശാസ്ത്രജ്ഞൻ	ആണ്	യാൻ	ടിൻബർജെൻ
Other	**Other**	**Other**	**Other**
Other	Other	Person	Person

Jan Tinbergen is a Dutch Economist

(5)

Tokens:	ശ്രീലങ്കൻ	ക്രിക്കറ്റ്	ചരിത്രത്തിലെ
ARNEKT:	**Other**	**Other**	**Person**
Prediction:	Place	Person	Other

ഏറ്റവും	മികച്ച	താരങ്ങളിലൊരാളാണ്	മുരളി
Other	**Other**	**Other**	**Person**
Other	Other	Other	Person

Murali is one of the best players in the history of Sri Lankan cricket

For CUSAT, the presence of out-of-domain/unseen words is clearly the cause of most errors in the vanilla model. Once fine-tuned with a portion of the data set, this is reduced significantly.

Disregarding the "Other" class, the model seems to confuse "Person" and "Organization" entites with "Place" entities in both data sets. This is almost always observed with multi worded entities that have places embedded in their names. Cases include people with places attached to them (as explained in section 5.3.1) and organizations with the same characteristic (e.g. "New York Public Library"). The "New York" portion in such entities can be thought of as a place entity embedded in an organization entity, or can be viewed simply as an organization entity without taking into account embedded entity classes. For one-worded entities, errors can often be seen to arise from annotation variations between the ground truth and the automatically generated dataset. For example, words such as “Library” and “College” are mapped as ”Place” entities by the Google Knowledge graph during the generation of title lists. Subsequently, instances of such words are labeled as ”Place” by our vanilla model trained on the WikiML dataset. However, the external datasets label them as ”Organization” entities in some cases, which indirectly translates to mistakes during evaluation.

8 Conclusion

We demonstrated the implementation of a fully automated pipeline for the creation of a named entity tagged data set with freely available resources. We showed how the pipeline can be adaptated for two morphologically complex, agglutinating languages. Finally, we propose an easily portable, weakly supervised NER system for Malayalam and isiZulu based on this pipeline. The system can be developed quickly: We spent 2 weeks on developing the initial system for Malayalam and 2 days for porting it to isiZulu. We tested in- and out-of-domain on a number of publicly available data sets, with encouraging results, especially for Malayalam.

References

A.P Ajees and Sumam Mary Idicula. 2018. A named entity recognition system for Malayalam using neural networks. *Procedia Computer Science*, 143:962 – 969. 8th International Conference on Advances in Computing & Communications (ICACC-2018).

K. K. Akhil, R. Rajimol, and V. S. Anoop. 2020. Parts-of-speech tagging for Malayalam using deep learning techniques. *International Journal of Information Technology*.

Mahathi Bhagavatula, Santosh GSK, and Vasudeva Varma. 2012. Language independent named entity identification using Wikipedia. In *Proceedings of the First Workshop on Multilingual Modeling*, pages 11–17, Jeju, Republic of Korea. Association for Computational Linguistics.

Premjith Bhavukam, Soman K.P., and M Anand Kumar. 2018. A deep learning approach for Malayalam morphological analysis at character level. *Procedia Computer Science*, 132:47 – 54. International Conference on Computational Intelligence and Data Science.

MS Bindu and Sumam Mary Idicula. 2011. Named entity identifier for Malayalam using linguistic principles employing statistical methods. *International Journal of Computer Science Issues(IJCSI)*, 8(5):185–191.

Dhouha Bouamor, Adrian Popescu, Nasredine Semmar, and Pierre Zweigenbaum. 2013. Building specialized bilingual lexicons using large scale background knowledge. In *Proceedings of the 2013 Conference on Empirical Methods in Natural Language Processing*, pages 479–489, Seattle, Washington, USA. Association for Computational Linguistics.

Alex Brandsen, Suzan Verberne, Milco Wansleeben, and Karsten Lambers. 2020. Creating a dataset for named entity recognition in the archaeology domain. In *Proceedings of the 12th Language Resources and Evaluation Conference*, pages 4573–4577, Marseille, France. European Language Resources Association.

Thorsten Brants. 2002. TnT: A statistical part-of-speech tagger. *ANLP*.

Jason P.C. Chiu and Eric Nichols. 2016. Named entity recognition with bidirectional LSTM-CNNs. *Transactions of the Association for Computational Linguistics*, 4:357–370.

François Chollet. 2015. Keras. `https://keras.io`.

Alexis Conneau, Kartikay Khandelwal, Naman Goyal, Vishrav Chaudhary, Guillaume Wenzek, Francisco Guzmán, Edouard Grave, Myle Ott, Luke Zettlemoyer, and Veselin Stoyanov. 2019. Unsupervised cross-lingual representation learning at scale. *arXiv preprint arXiv:1911.02116*.

G. Remmiya Devi, P.V. Veena, M. Anand Kumar, and K.P. Soman. 2016. Entity extraction for Malayalam social media text using structured skip-gram based embedding features from unlabeled data. *Procedia Computer Science*, 93:547 – 553. Proceedings of the 6th International Conference on Advances in Computing and Communications.

Roald Eiselen. 2016. Government domain named entity recognition for South African languages. In *Proceedings of the Tenth International Conference on Language Resources and Evaluation (LREC'16)*, pages 3344–3348.

Christiane Fellbaum, editor. 1998. *WordNet: An Electronic Lexical Database*. MIT Press, Cambridge, MA.

Barathi Ganesh Hullathy Balakrishnan, Soman KP, Reshma U, Mandar Kale, Prachi Mankame, Gouri Kulkarni, Anitha Kale, and Anand Kumar M. 2018. Information extraction for conversational systems in Indian languages - Arnekt IECSIL. In *Proceedings of the 10th Annual Meeting of the Forum for Information Retrieval Evaluation*, FIRE'18, page 18–20, New York, NY, USA. Association for Computing Machinery.

Jun'ichi Kazama and Kentaro Torisawa. 2007. Exploiting Wikipedia as external knowledge for named entity recognition. In *Proceedings of the 2007 Joint Conference on Empirical Methods in Natural Language Processing and Computational Natural Language Learning (EMNLP-CoNLL)*, pages 698–707, Prague, Czech Republic. Association for Computational Linguistics.

Steven Krauwer. 2003. The Basic Language Resource Kit (BLARK) as the first milestone for the language resources roadmap. In *Proceedings of the 2003 International Workshop Speech and Computer (SPECOM 2003)*, pages 8–15.

S. Kumar, M. Anand Kumar, and K.P. Soman. 2019. Deep learning based part-of-speech tagging for Malayalam Twitter data (special issue: Deep learning techniques for natural language processing). *Journal of Intelligent Systems*, 28(3):423 – 435.

Patrick Littell, Kartik Goyal, David R. Mortensen, Alexa Little, Chris Dyer, and Lori Levin. 2016. Named entity recognition for linguistic rapid response in low-resource languages: Sorani Kurdish and Tajik. In *Proceedings of COLING 2016, the 26th International Conference on Computational Linguistics: Technical Papers*, pages 998–1006, Osaka, Japan. The COLING 2016 Organizing Committee.

Ilya Loshchilov and Frank Hutter. 2019. Decoupled weight decay regularization. In *International Conference on Learning Representations*.

Stephen Mayhew, Chen-Tse Tsai, and Dan Roth. 2017. Cheap translation for cross-lingual named entity recognition. In *Proceedings of the 2017 Conference on Empirical Methods in Natural Language Processing*, pages 2536–2545, Copenhagen, Denmark. Association for Computational Linguistics.

S. K. Nambiar, A. Leons, S. Jose, and Arunsree. 2019. POS tagger for Malayalam using Hidden Markov Model. In *2019 International Conference on Smart Systems and Inventive Technology (ICSSIT)*, pages 957–960.

Jian Ni and Radu Florian. 2016. Improving multilingual named entity recognition with Wikipedia entity type mapping. In *Proceedings of the 2016 Conference on Empirical Methods in Natural Language Processing*, pages 1275–1284, Austin, Texas. Association for Computational Linguistics.

Joel Nothman, James R. Curran, and Tara Murphy. 2008. Transforming Wikipedia into named entity training data. In *Proceedings of the Australasian Language Technology Association Workshop 2008*, pages 124–132, Hobart, Australia.

Joel Nothman, Tara Murphy, and James R. Curran. 2009. Analysing Wikipedia and gold-standard corpora for NER training. In *Proceedings of the 12th Conference of the European Chapter of the ACL (EACL 2009)*, pages 612–620, Athens, Greece. Association for Computational Linguistics.

Jisha P Jayan, Rajeev R R, and Elizabeth Sherly. 2013. A hybrid statistical approach for named entity recognition for Malayalam language. In *Proceedings of the 11th Workshop on Asian Language Resources*, pages 58–63, Nagoya, Japan. Asian Federation of Natural Language Processing.

Xiaoman Pan, Boliang Zhang, Jonathan May, Joel Nothman, Kevin Knight, and Heng Ji. 2017. Cross-lingual name tagging and linking for 282 languages. In *Proceedings of the 55th Annual Meeting of the Association for Computational Linguistics (Volume 1: Long Papers)*, pages 1946–1958, Vancouver, Canada. Association for Computational Linguistics.

Will Radford, Xavier Carreras, and James Henderson. 2015. Named entity recognition with document-specific KB tag gazetteers. In *Proceedings of the 2015 Conference on Empirical Methods in Natural Language Processing*, pages 512–517, Lisbon, Portugal. Association for Computational Linguistics.

Lev Ratinov and Dan Roth. 2009. Design challenges and misconceptions in named entity recognition. In *Proceedings of the Thirteenth Conference on Computational Natural Language Learning (CoNLL-2009)*, pages 147–155, Boulder, Colorado. Association for Computational Linguistics.

Alexander E. Richman and Patrick Schone. 2008. Mining Wiki resources for multilingual named entity recognition. In *Proceedings of ACL-08: HLT*, pages 1–9, Columbus, Ohio. Association for Computational Linguistics.

S. Shruthi, Jiljo, and P.V. Pranav. 2016. A study on named entity recognition for Malayalam language using TnT tagger & maximum entropy Markov model. *International Journal of Applied Engineering Research*, 11:5425–5429.

Amit Singhal. 2012. Introducing the Knowledge Graph: things, not strings. https://www.blog.google/products/search/introducing-knowledge-graph-things-not/.

P S Sreeja and Anitha S Pillai. 2020. Towards an efficient Malayalam named entity recognizer analysis on the challenges. *Procedia Computer Science*, 171:2541 – 2546. Third International Conference on Computing and Network Communications (CoCoNet'19).

Chi Sun, Xipeng Qiu, Yige Xu, and Xuanjing Huang. 2019. How to fine-tune bert for text classification? In *Chinese Computational Linguistics*, pages 194–206, Cham. Springer International Publishing.

Elsabé Taljard and Sonja E. Bosch. 2006. A comparison of approaches to word class tagging: Disjunctively vs. conjunctively written Bantu languages. *Nordic journal of African studies*, 15(4):428–442.

Antonio Toral and Rafael Muñoz. 2006. A proposal to automatically build and maintain gazetteers for named entity recognition by using Wikipedia. In *Proceedings of the Workshop on NEW TEXT Wikis and blogs and other dynamic text sources*.

Semi-Automated Labeling of Requirement Datasets for Relation Extraction

Jeremias Bohn
Technical University of Munich, Germany
jeremias.bohn@tum.de

Jannik Fischbach
Qualicen GmbH, Germany
jannik.fischbach@qualicen.de

Martin Schmitt
Center for Information and Language Processing
LMU Munich, Germany
martin@cis.lmu.de

Hinrich Schütze
Center for Information and Language Processing
LMU Munich, Germany
inquiries@cislmu.org

Andreas Vogelsang
University of Cologne, Germany
vogelsang@cis.uni-koeln.de

Abstract

Creating datasets manually by human annotators is a laborious task that can lead to biased and inhomogeneous labels. We propose a flexible, semi-automatic framework for labeling data for relation extraction. Furthermore, we provide a dataset of preprocessed sentences from the requirements engineering domain, including a set of automatically created as well as hand-crafted labels. In our case study, we compare the human and automatic labels and show that there is a substantial overlap between both annotations.

1 Introduction

While recent advances in Natural Language Processing have yielded high-quality language models such as BERT (Devlin et al., 2019), GPT-3 (Brown et al., 2020) and ELECTRA (Clark et al., 2020) which are able to continue sentences, fill in masked words and correctly parse human language, using these models for most use-case scenarios still requires them to be trained on a down-stream task using labeled data. For some tasks, e.g. sentiment analysis of reviews, creating datasets is relatively easy as large databases with annotations already exist (such as the IMDb movie review dataset (Maas et al., 2011)). However, training a model on niche tasks often demands hand-crafting new datasets from spread-out documents. This is usually done by humans who collect, preprocess, and annotate sentences which is a laborious task and can result in biased and/or inhomogeneous labeling, e.g. if annotation instructions were not understood correctly or left room for subjective interpretation. This becomes especially apparent if multiple, non-expert individuals are involved in this process.

In requirements engineering, we usually work with large documents written in natural language (Mich et al., 2004; Kassab et al., 2014) which describe the specifications of a software project, usually classified as either functional requirements, specifying what functionality the system should provide, and non-functional requirements, specifying in what way the system should implement those functions. However, these documents are often updated during the life cycle of the project and span up to multiple hundreds of pages, depending on the project size. Keeping track of all the changes and maintaining the software based on the requirement document can soon become a challenge (Fischbach et al., 2020) which is why an automatic conversion to, e.g., UML diagrams can come in handy. To do so, it is necessary to parse the relations between entities from the written text into a structured format, thus creating a comparable corpus of requirements in natural language and the same relation in a formal language.

In this paper, we propose a semi-automatic approach that, given a clean, grammatically correct sentence stating a software requirement, outputs a labeling corresponding to the relation the requirement describes based on a small set of pre-defined rules of word dependency relations. This should reduce human bias manifesting in labels as the annotator does not actively choose the labels for each word anymore but instead defines abstract rules

Proceedings of 14th Workshop on Building and Using Comparable Corpora in conjunction with RANLP-2021, pages 40–45, held online, 6 September 2021.
https://doi.org/10.26615/978-954-452-076-2_006

which provide for homogeneous, deterministic labeling and reduce the amount of labor for creating such datasets. This automatically annotated data can then be used for training a more powerful model, as shown by Schmitt et al. (2020).
We summarize our main contributions as follows:

- We provide a high-quality, preprocessed dataset of 2,093 requirement sentences together with 1,848 automatically created labels and another 199 manually created labels for a subset of the automatically labeled sentences as a resource for further research projects.

- We provide a flexible, semi-automatic framework for data annotation of the relation extraction domain based on dependency parsing and pattern matching.

- We conduct a case study on the said framework on requirement document sentences, showing its annotation results are matching those of humans to a substantial degree.

2 Related Work

Gamallo et al. (2012) propose a simple Open Information Extraction system based on dependency parse trees. The algorithm extracts triples with two arguments and a sentence part relating those. However, the patterns are not very sophisticated and put a large part of the sentence into the relation. Hence, this approach is not suitable for our use case as we would eventually like to generate object diagrams from the relations we extracted. Erkan et al. (2007) use dependency parse trees to extract relations between proteins from sentences. They do so by classifying whether a sentence, given a dependency tree, describes a relation between any pair of proteins occurring in the sentence using semi-supervised harmonic functions and support vector machines. However, their entities (the protein names) are already annotated which is not the case if we only have the raw sentences as in our approach. Mausam et al. (2012) use dependency trees and a labeled bootstrap dataset to automatically generate patterns for information extraction, unlike our approach which does not require to annotate any data manually but instead to produce patterns. While this approach might be able to extract simple triples well, one needs either a larger annotated dataset, defeating the purpose of our work, or the patterns might not generalize well, thus being unsuitable for constructing a qualitative annotated corpus. Reddy et al. (2016) propose an algorithm to automatically extract logical expressions from dependency parse trees for question answering. These were then converted into a graph indicating the relations between the named entities in the sentence by applying semantic parsing. However, this approach always converts the entire sentence into a graph and may include information that is irrelevant for a dataset that is to be generated. Inago et al. (2019) use a rule-based approach on dependency trees to process natural language car parking instructions with decision trees for automated driving systems. Unlike our data (or most datasets in general), sentences of the application domain are very short and similar in structure. While our approach could be effectively converted into a decision tree, it is easier to construct rules with our pattern engine for more complex data.

3 Corpus Creation

3.1 Dataset

For our dataset, we use 19 publicly available requirement documents in the English language from the PURE dataset (Ferrari et al., 2017), with a large topical variety, including governmental institution software in military and scientific fields, inventory management systems and video games. All documents are provided in .PDF, .HTML or .DOC format. From these, we manually extracted 2,104 requirement sentences (1,639 functional, 465 non-functional requirements).

3.2 Preprocessing

As we want to automatically dependency parse our sentences, we have to ensure that all input to the model is grammatically and orthographically sound. We also have to ensure that any unnecessary information is removed to not confuse the parser. Therefore, we manually applied the following formatting operations to each sentence during data extraction:

- Splitting of enumerations into multiple sentences, adjusting words if necessary to make the sentence sound (e.g., nounification of verbs); e.g., "The system has to include a) [...] b) [...] c) [...]" becomes 3 sentences, each including exactly one of the requirements

- Removal of extra inter-punctuation (additional spaces, dots, commas, etc.)

- Removal of references to sections, tables, figures, or other requirements of the document as they are not relevant for extracting the relation of the sentence itself
- Removal of abbreviations after written-out expressions (e.g., in "automated teller machine (ATM)", the "(ATM)" is dropped)
- Removal of requirement reference numbers
- Correction of spelling mistakes where obvious
- Adding of dots at the end of each sentence if missing
- Changing the first letter of a sentence to upper case if it is not yet
- Removal of quotation marks around pseudo-correct terms (e.g., 'the "processor" will [...]' becomes 'the processor will [...]')
- Removal of explicit explanations of what is included in some term (e.g., "errors of either kind, i.e. hardware and software, [...]")
- Lower-casing of words if they are not abbreviations (e.g., "NOT" becomes "not")
- Remove brackets around additional plural 's' (e.g., "socket(s)" becomes "sockets")
- Exchanging "/" with "and" or "or" where applicable and possible given the context (e.g. "The system should support adding/deleting files" becomes "The system should support adding and deleting files")
- Unification of the possessive 's' preceding symbols ("'" and "´" are changed to "'")
- Removal of duplicate sentences (11 in total)

After these preprocessing steps, the average sentence length is 19.87 words, the maximum is 69 words and the minimum 4 words.

3.3 Labeling

These final 2,093 sentences (1,628 functional, 465 non-functional requirements) are parsed to extract dependencies using the Neural Adobe-UCSD Parser (Mrini et al., 2020) which achieved state-of-the-art performance on the Penn Treebank dataset (Marcus et al., 1993). Based on these dependencies, we handcraft a total of 102 patterns to label 91.03% of the functional and 78.71% of the non-functional sentences without any further human interaction. Each pattern is a sequence of triples (l, dp, c) where l is a label, dp a sequence of dependency labels forming a path downwards a dependency tree and c a Boolean value indicating whether all children (direct and indirect) should be left out from labeling or not. Each sequence applies all or a subset of the following entity tags to the sentences:

- `ent1`: The main entity of the requirement. Either the acting component or the component on which a constraint is applied (if there is no second entity)
- `rel`: The relation/action of the requirement.
- `ent2`: The passive entity of the requirement. Either the component on which an action is performed or which is involved in the action passively
- `cond`: Any modifier of the requirement. Can further specify the requirement or put conditions on it how or when it will be applied.

An excerpt of automatic annotations can be found in Table 1. Each pattern is applied using tree traversal: for each label that is to be applied, a sequence of dependency labels (optionally with modifiers) is given, starting at the root. The algorithm checks whether the current nodes have any direct children connected to them with the current dependency label of the sequence. If so, we check whether these children have children connected to them with the next label in the sequence. If not, the pattern fitting is stopped and no labeling is applied to the sentence. If we reach the end of the sequence, the final node is labeled with the given label and, depending on a parameter, all of its children, too. A simple example can be found in Table 2, row 1. Dependency labels can include modifiers to allow for more complex patterns:

- Starting with `!`, the pattern matching will remove any node that has one or more children with the given dependency label. Thus, no step downwards the tree is taken
- Followed by `=[placeholder]` where `[placeholder]` is any word, only those nodes are considered where the label is the given label and the actual word of the node is specified by `[placeholder]`

Sentence
While flying two MAE AVs Beyond Line Of Sight $_{\texttt{cond}}$, the TCS $_{\texttt{ent1}}$ shall provide $_{\texttt{rel}}$ full control functionality $_{\texttt{ent2}}$ of each AV $_{\texttt{cond}}$.
NPAC SMS $_{\texttt{ent1}}$ shall default $_{\texttt{rel}}$ the EDR Indicator $_{\texttt{ent2}}$ to False $_{\texttt{cond}}$.
A bulk entry $_{\texttt{ent1}}$ can be used to add $_{\texttt{rel}}$ many assets $_{\texttt{ent2}}$.
The HATS-GUI $_{\texttt{ent1}}$ shall interact with the Host OS to compare $_{\texttt{rel}}$ time stamps $_{\texttt{ent2}}$ for files $_{\texttt{cond}}$.
The BE $_{\texttt{ent1}}$ shall be able to apply $_{\texttt{rel}}$ corrections $_{\texttt{ent2}}$ based on state count and/or quantizer power measurement data $_{\texttt{cond}}$.

Table 1: Examples of Labeling

- .. lets us traverse back to the parent of the current node. This allows us to check nodes for their existence without including them in the actual labeling

A selection of patterns used can be found in Table 2. In our setting, one sentence usually holds one relation, however, this is not the case for conjunctions of multiple main clauses or instructions. Due to current limitations of our engine (see Section 6), the relation of the first main clause is always chosen, however, this depends on the pattern design. Even though we only use requirements written in English, a large portion of the rules could be applied to data in different languages as the Universal Dependencies (Schuster and Manning, 2016) rely on the concept of primacy of content, allowing for very similar dependency trees. However, patterns explicitly using keywords may not generalize well for other languages. The code for the labeling task as well as the labeled data can be found on GitHub[1].

4 Evaluation

Given our automatically labeled data, we evaluate the quality of the labels by comparing its output to human annotations. To do so, we randomly sample 199 sentences (10.77%) from the 1848 sentences which were automatically labeled. Two of the authors then annotated these sentences manually. The annotators were given the descriptions of each label type, but had no access to the actual labeling from the algorithm. Annotators collaboratively labeled the data, discussing the labeling for each sentence and agreeing upon a single valid labeling. We then calculate inter-rater reliability with the Cohen's κ between the human annotators and the automatic annotator, once over all labels and once as average inter-reliability per sentence (i.e., we calculate one Cohen's κ score per sentence and average over all sentences –this considers each sentence equally while the overall score puts more weight on longer sentences). The results can be found in Table 3. While the overall score puts more weight on long sentences, the sentence average provides us an approximation of the reliability of our automatic annotator for any sentence. According to the taxonomy of Landis and Koch (Landis and Koch, 1977), the per sentence average κ value indicates a substantial inter-annotator agreement, the overall κ a moderate agreement. While the main acting entity is extracted very well with almost perfect agreement according to Landis and Koch, extracting relational modifiers proofs to be the hardest with only moderate agreement between our automatic approach and the human annotators. This is mostly due to the nature of the label itself, spanning a large variety of modifiers from conditions to entities not involved in the relation itself. While one could split the `cond` label into multiple different labels, this would increase the number of patterns required a lot. Alternatively, one might reduce the coverage of the labeling in general but we focused on including as much information as possible. The relatively low score for `ent2` mainly arises from sentences containing multiple relations where many words describe a passive entity for other relations than the one of the main sentence. Our approach currently is not able to effectively extract multiple relations from a single sentence yet. This is also the reason why the score `rel` is lower than the one for `ent1`.

5 Limitations

While our approach works well for requirements documents - after all, relations between software entities and modifications of these relations can be extracted well by syntactically parsing the sentence structure - this does not apply to word labels which require a semantic understanding of the input. For example, if we were to create labels for Named Entity Recognition, our algorithm would fail as

[1] `https://github.com/JeremiasBohn/RequirementRelationExtractor`

Pattern	Description
('rel', ['root'], True) ('ent1', ['root', 'nsubj'], False) ('ent2', ['root', 'dobj'], False) ('cond', ['root', 'advcl'], False)	Simple pattern, sets the root of the sentence as the relation (only this single word), the entire nominal subject as the acting entity, the entire direct object as the passive entity. An adverbial clause is treated as a relation modifier.
('rel', ['root=capable', 'prep=of', 'pcomp'], True) ('ent1', ['root', 'nsubj'], False) ('ent2', ['root', 'prep=of', 'pcomp', 'prep=in', 'pobj'], False) ('cond', ['root', 'advcl'], False)	Catches phrases like "The system should be capable of [...]" and searches for the passive entity in the prepositional object of the prepositional clause starting with "in".
('rel', ['root', '!dobj'], True) ('ent1', ['root', 'nsubjpass'], False) ('cond', ['root', 'prep=in', 'pobj=case', '..'], False) ('cond', ['root', 'advmod'], False)	Pattern is only applied if the sentence has no direct object (which could serve as the passive entity). Prepositional sentences starting with "in case" are labeled as requirement modifier (we have to traverse the tree upwards again to include the 'in' as well).

Table 2: Examples of Patterns

Labels considered	Sentence Avg.	Overall
All labels	0.632	0.576
`rel` only	0.790	0.720
`ent1` only	0.855	0.822
`ent2` only	0.619	0.561
`cond` only	0.532	0.543

Table 3: Cohen's Kappa Results

it is not possible to find syntactic rules to distinguish between, e.g., an organization and a person. Also, the algorithm fails in some cases if either rules are not specific enough or the dependency parser mistakenly adds dependencies between sentence parts where there is no dependency between them. The latter may especially occur frequently if the sentences were not preprocessed well which is why our algorithm is not suitable as a classifier in general (if we, on the other hand, use our data as training input for a Transformer model (Vaswani et al., 2017), it may overcome these strict syntactic requirements and generalize better on real-world data).

6 Conclusion & Outlook

In this paper, we present a novel approach for data labeling which allows users to annotate sentences for relation extraction within a shorter time period compared to manual annotation while at the same time having a consistent labeling scheme for the entire dataset. Our approach exploits syntactic features which are the integral foundation of most relation extraction tasks.

For the future, it would be helpful to implement an automatic extraction of requirement sentences by, e.g., training a classifier to identify relevant sentences in plain text or .PDF documents as well as a semi-automatic approach with human validation for preprocessing sentences into grammatically and orthographically sound ones. We plan on extending the pattern engine our algorithm relies on, e.g., allowing for recursive patterns to parse nested sentences and to extract multiple relations from one sentence as well as optional pattern parts to reduce redundancy (e.g., a sentence where the active entity is the nominal subject, the relation the dependency tree root and the passive entity the direct object may have a relation modifier in an adverbial clause. As of the current state, this requires two patterns (exponentially increasing with the number of optional dependencies) while with a pattern where this adverbial clause is considered optional, we only need a single pattern).

References

Tom B Brown, Benjamin Mann, Nick Ryder, Melanie Subbiah, Jared Kaplan, Prafulla Dhariwal, Arvind Neelakantan, Pranav Shyam, Girish Sastry, Amanda Askell, et al. 2020. Language models are few-shot learners. *arXiv preprint arXiv:2005.14165*.

Kevin Clark, Minh-Thang Luong, Quoc V Le, and Christopher D Manning. 2020. Electra: Pre-training text encoders as discriminators rather than generators. *arXiv preprint arXiv:2003.10555*.

Jacob Devlin, Ming-Wei Chang, Kenton Lee, and Kristina Toutanova. 2019. BERT: Pre-training of deep bidirectional transformers for language understanding. In *Proceedings of the 2019 Conference of the North American Chapter of the Association for Computational Linguistics: Human Language Technologies, Volume 1 (Long and Short Papers)*, pages 4171–4186, Minneapolis, Minnesota. Association for Computational Linguistics.

Güneş Erkan, Arzucan Özgür, and Dragomir R. Radev. 2007. Semi-supervised classification for extracting protein interaction sentences using dependency parsing. In *Proceedings of the 2007 Joint Conference on Empirical Methods in Natural Language Processing and Computational Natural Language Learning (EMNLP-CoNLL)*, pages 228–237, Prague, Czech Republic. Association for Computational Linguistics.

Alessio Ferrari, Giorgio Oronzo Spagnolo, and Stefania Gnesi. 2017. Pure: A dataset of public requirements documents. In *2017 IEEE 25th International Requirements Engineering Conference (RE)*, pages 502–505.

Jannik Fischbach, Henning Femmer, Daniel Mendez, Davide Fucci, and Andreas Vogelsang. 2020. What makes agile test artifacts useful? an activity-based quality model from a practitioners' perspective. In *Proceedings of the 14th ACM / IEEE International Symposium on Empirical Software Engineering and Measurement (ESEM)*, ESEM '20, New York, NY, USA. Association for Computing Machinery.

Pablo Gamallo, Marcos Garcia, and Santiago Fernández-Lanza. 2012. Dependency-based open information extraction. In *Proceedings of the Joint Workshop on Unsupervised and Semi-Supervised Learning in NLP*, pages 10–18, Avignon, France. Association for Computational Linguistics.

Akari Inago, Hiroshi Tsukahara, and Ichiro Kobayashi. 2019. Parsing parking instructions for self-driving cars into spatial semantic descriptions. *J. Comput.*, 14(5):328–338.

Mohamad Kassab, Colin Neill, and Phillip Laplante. 2014. State of practice in requirements engineering: contemporary data. *Innovations in Systems and Software Engineering*.

J. Richard Landis and Gary G. Koch. 1977. The measurement of observer agreement for categorical data. *Biometrics*, 33(1):159–174.

Andrew L. Maas, Raymond E. Daly, Peter T. Pham, Dan Huang, Andrew Y. Ng, and Christopher Potts. 2011. Learning word vectors for sentiment analysis. In *Proceedings of the 49th Annual Meeting of the Association for Computational Linguistics: Human Language Technologies*, pages 142–150, Portland, Oregon, USA. Association for Computational Linguistics.

Mitchell P. Marcus, Beatrice Santorini, and Mary Ann Marcinkiewicz. 1993. Building a large annotated corpus of English: The Penn Treebank. *Computational Linguistics*, 19(2):313–330.

Mausam, Michael Schmitz, Stephen Soderland, Robert Bart, and Oren Etzioni. 2012. Open language learning for information extraction. In *Proceedings of the 2012 Joint Conference on Empirical Methods in Natural Language Processing and Computational Natural Language Learning*, pages 523–534, Jeju Island, Korea. Association for Computational Linguistics.

Luisa Mich, Mariangela Franch, and Pierluigi Novi Inverardi. 2004. Market research for requirements analysis using linguistic tools. *Requirements Engineering*.

Khalil Mrini, Franck Dernoncourt, Quan Hung Tran, Trung Bui, Walter Chang, and Ndapa Nakashole. 2020. Rethinking self-attention: Towards interpretability in neural parsing. In *Findings of the Association for Computational Linguistics: EMNLP 2020*, pages 731–742, Online. Association for Computational Linguistics.

Siva Reddy, Oscar Täckström, Michael Collins, Tom Kwiatkowski, Dipanjan Das, Mark Steedman, and Mirella Lapata. 2016. Transforming dependency structures to logical forms for semantic parsing. *Transactions of the Association for Computational Linguistics*, 4:127–140.

Martin Schmitt, Sahand Sharifzadeh, Volker Tresp, and Hinrich Schütze. 2020. An unsupervised joint system for text generation from knowledge graphs and semantic parsing. In *Proceedings of the 2020 Conference on Empirical Methods in Natural Language Processing (EMNLP)*, pages 7117–7130, Online. Association for Computational Linguistics.

Sebastian Schuster and Christopher D. Manning. 2016. Enhanced English Universal Dependencies: An improved representation for natural language understanding tasks. In *Proceedings of the Tenth International Conference on Language Resources and Evaluation (LREC'16)*, pages 2371–2378, Portorož, Slovenia. European Language Resources Association (ELRA).

Ashish Vaswani, Noam Shazeer, Niki Parmar, Jakob Uszkoreit, Llion Jones, Aidan N Gomez, Łukasz Kaiser, and Illia Polosukhin. 2017. Attention is all you need. In *Advances in neural information processing systems*, pages 5998–6008.

Majority Voting with Bidirectional Pre-translation For Bitext Retrieval

Alex Jones
Dartmouth College
alexander.g.jones.23@dartmouth.edu

Derry Tanti Wijaya
Boston University
wijaya@bu.edu

Abstract

Obtaining high-quality parallel corpora is of paramount importance for training NMT systems. However, as many language pairs lack adequate gold-standard training data, a popular approach has been to mine so-called "pseudo-parallel" sentences from paired documents in two languages. In this paper, we outline some drawbacks with current methods that rely on an embedding similarity threshold, and propose a heuristic method in its place. Our method involves *translating both halves of a paired corpus before mining*, and then performing a majority vote on sentence pairs mined in three ways: after translating documents in language $x \rightarrow$ language y, after translating $y \rightarrow x$, and using the original documents in languages x and y. We demonstrate success with this novel approach on the Tatoeba similarity search benchmark in 64 low-resource languages, and on NMT in Kazakh and Gujarati. We also uncover the effect of *resource-related factors* (i.e. how much monolingual/bilingual data is available for a given language) on the *optimal choice of bitext mining method*, demonstrating that there is currently no one-size-fits-all approach for this task. We make the code and data used in our experiments publicly available.[1]

1 Introduction

Mining so-called "pseudo-parallel" sentences from sets of similar documents in different languages ("comparable corpora") has gained popularity in recent years as a means of overcoming the dearth of parallel training data for many language pairs. With increasingly powerful computational resources and highly efficient tools such as `Faiss` (Johnson et al., 2017) at our disposal, the possibility of mining billions of pseudo-parallel bitexts for thousands of language pairs to the end of training a multilingual NMT system has been realized. For example, Fan et al. (2020) perform global mining over billions of sentences in 100 languages, resulting in a massively multilingual NMT system that supports supervised translation in 2200 directions.

Despite these breakthroughs in high-resource engineering, many questions remain to be answered about bitext mining from a research perspective, with particular attention directed toward the *low-resource engineering case*, i.e. research settings with limited computational resources. While Fan et al. (2020) yield impressive results using hundreds of GPUs, aggressive computational optimization, and a global bitext mining procedure (i.e. searching the entire target corpus for a source sentence match), how these results transfer to the low computational resource case is not clear. Moreover, the effect of circumstantial (e.g. the resources available for a given language or language pair) or linguistic (e.g. typological) factors on bitext mining performance remains highly understudied.

In light of these issues, our contributions are as follows:

- We demonstrate the problematic nature of using similarity-score-based thresholding for mining bitexts, with particular attention given to document-level mining of low-resource languages.
- We propose a novel, heuristic approach for bitext mining that involves translating both halves of a bilingual corpus, mining with three sets of documents (two distinct translated pairs of documents plus the original documents), and then performing a majority vote on the resulting sentence pairs. This approach avoids the pitfalls of laboriously tuning a similarity score threshold, a practice we believe to have been weakly motivated in past studies.

[1] https://github.com/AlexJonesNLP/alt-bitexts

Proceedings of 14th Workshop on Building and Using Comparable Corpora in conjunction with RANLP-2021, pages 46–59, held online, 6 September 2021.
https://doi.org/10.26615/978-954-452-076-2_007

- We show the success of our method on NMT in English-Kazakh and English-Gujarati, and also on the gold-standard bitext retrieval task ("similarity search" on the Tatoeba dataset), and show the optimal choice of mining approach to be partially dependent on the resource availability of the language(s) involved.

2 Related Work

Mining pseudo-parallel sentences from paired corpora for the purpose of training NMT systems is a decades-old problem, and dozens of solutions have been tried, ranging from statistical or heuristic-based approaches (Zhao and Vogel, 2002; Resnik and Smith, 2003; Munteanu et al., 2004; Fung and Cheung, 2004; Munteanu and Marcu, 2006) to similarity-based, rule-based, and hybrid approaches (Azpeitia et al., 2017, 2018; Bouamor and Sajjad, 2018; Hangya et al., 2018; Schwenk, 2018; Ramesh and Sankaranarayanan, 2018; Artetxe and Schwenk, 2019a,b; Hangya and Fraser, 2019; Schwenk et al., 2019a,b; Wu et al., 2019; Keung et al., 2020; Tran et al., 2020; Kvapilíková et al., 2020; Feng et al., 2020; Fan et al., 2020). Benchmarks to measure performance on this task include the BUCC[2] '17/18 datasets (Zweigenbaum et al., 2017, 2018), whose task involves spotting gold-standard bitexts within comparable corpora, and the Tatoeba dataset (Artetxe and Schwenk, 2019b), whose task involves matching gold-standard pairs in truly parallel corpora.

Relevant to similarity-based mining methods are well-aligned cross-lingual word and sentence embeddings, which are some of the oldest constructs in NLP and have been tackled using hundreds of diverse approaches. Even among relatively recent efforts, these approaches range from static, monolingual embeddings (Pennington et al., 2014; Mikolov et al., 2013; Arora et al., 2017; Kiros et al., 2015) to static, multilingual ones (Klementiev et al., 2012; Ammar et al., 2016; Schwenk and Douze, 2017) to contextualized, monolingual ones (Peters et al., 2018; Subramanian et al., 2018; Devlin et al., 2019; Liu et al., 2019; Conneau et al., 2017; Reimers and Gurevych, 2019) to contextualized, multilingual ones (Song et al., 2019; Conneau et al., 2020; Reimers and Gurevych, 2020; Feng et al., 2020; Wang et al., 2019). In this paper, our approach centers around using *contextualized, multilingual sentence* embeddings for the task of bitext mining.

For low-resource languages where parallel training data is little to none, unsupervised NMT can play a crucial role (Artetxe et al., 2018a, 2019a,b, 2018b; Hoang et al., 2018; Lample et al., 2017, 2018b,c; Pourdamghani et al., 2019; Wu et al., 2019). However, previous works have only focused on high-resource languages and/or languages that are typologically similar to English. Most recently, several works have questioned the universal usefulness of unsupervised NMT and showed its poor results for low-resource languages (Kim et al., 2020; Marchisio et al., 2020). They note the importance of typological similarity between source and target language, in addition to domain proximity and the size and quality of the monolingual corpora involved. They reason that since these conditions can hardly be satisfied in the case of low-resource languages, they result in poor unsupervised performance for these languages. However, recently it has been shown that training a language model on monolingual corpora, followed by training with an unsupervised MT objective, and then training on mined comparable data (Kuwanto et al., 2021) can improve MT performance for low-resource languages. In this work, we explore the usefulness of our mined bitext using a similar pipeline. We show an improvement over using only supervised training data for low-resource MT.

3 Model selection

3.1 Cross-lingual Sentence Embeddings

We initially experiment with XLM-RoBERTa (Conneau et al., 2020) for our bitext mining task, using averaged token embeddings (Keung et al., 2020) or the [CLS] (final) token embedding as makeshift sentence embeddings. However, we replicate results from Reimers and Gurevych (2020) in showing these ad-hoc sentence embeddings to have relatively poor performance on the BUCC '17/18 EN-FR train data (Zweigenbaum et al., 2017, 2018) compared to bona fide sentence embeddings like LASER (Artetxe and Schwenk, 2019b) and LaBSE (Feng et al., 2020). Thus, we opt to use LaBSE as our sentence embedding model, using its implementation in the Sentence Transformers [3] library. LaBSE performs state-of-the-art (SOTA) or near-SOTA on the BUCC and Tatoeba datasets

[2]Building and Using Comparable Corpora

[3]https://www.sbert.net

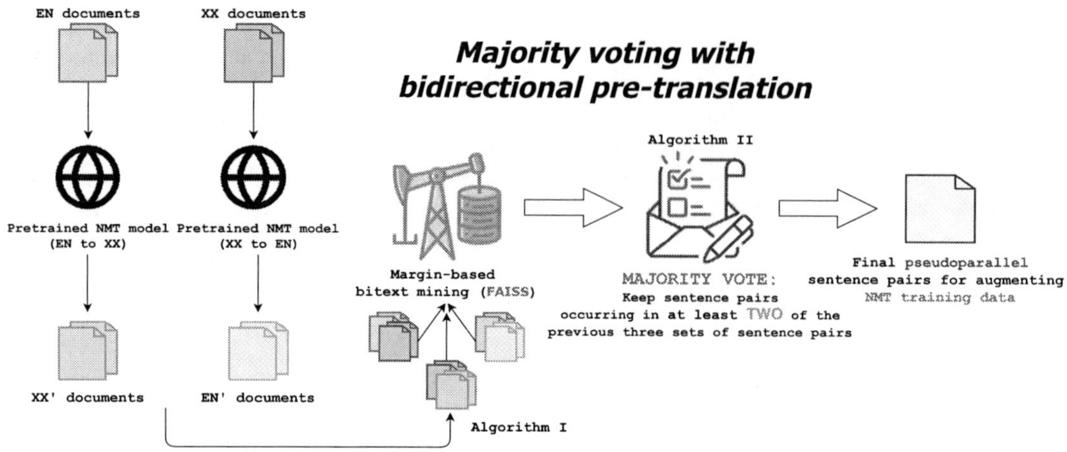

Figure 1: The pipeline we offer for selecting sentence translation pairs from comparable or parallel (e.g. Tatoeba) corpora using a heuristic voting approach. See Algorithms 1 and 2 for further details.

(Artetxe and Schwenk, 2019b)[4], and has demonstrated cross-lingual transfer capabilities for low-resource languages in particular. Moreover, being more recent than LASER, LaBSE has been investigated less thoroughly in the context of the bitext mining task.

4 Methods

An overview of our method for extracting bitexts is given in Figure 1; the processes are sketched in greater detail in Algorithms 1 and 2. The retrieval process begins with a set of English documents and a set of documents in another language XX. Both sets of documents are then translated using a pretrained NMT model to obtain XX' documents (English documents translated to XX) and EN' documents (XX documents translated to English).

We then perform margin-based translation mining (described below in Section 4.1 and in Algorithm 1) on three sets of documents: the original EN-XX documents, the EN-EN' documents, and the XX-XX' documents. Lastly, we perform a majority vote (see Algorithm 2, "majority voting") on the resulting sentence pairs, keeping any pair that occurs in $\geq$ 2 of the three sets of sentence pairs. If mined from a comparable corpus such as Wikipedia, these pseudoparallel sentence pairs can then be used to augment the training data of the pretrained NMT models, or (help) train an NMT model from scratch, as in Fan et al. (2020).

Alternative methods for filtering an initial set of sentence pairs are also given in Algorithm 2 (see comments in blue). Empirically, we find our majority voting method to be superior when a pretrained NMT model is available for both languages, while vanilla margin-based mining (Artetxe and Schwenk, 2019a) performs best in the absence of a pretrained NMT model. Results are discussed in greater detail in Section 6.

4.1 Primary retrieval procedure: Margin-based Mining

For our primary mining procedure, we use margin-based mining as described in Artetxe and Schwenk (2019a). Seeking to mitigate the hubness problem (Dinu et al., 2014), margin scoring poses an alternative to raw cosine similarity in that it selects the candidate embedding that "stands out" the most from its k nearest neighbors. We use the *ratio* margin score, as described in Artetxe and Schwenk (2019a) and defined below:

(1)

$$\text{score}(x, y) = \frac{\cos(x, y)}{\frac{1}{2k}\left(\sum_{z \in NN_k(x)} \cos(x, z) + \sum_{z \in NN_k(y)} \cos(y, z)\right)}$$

As in Artetxe and Schwenk (2019a), we use $k = 4$ for all our mining procedures. We acknowledge that k is indeed a tuneable and important hyperparameter of KNN search, and that higher values of k may work better for bitext mining in certain scenarios, depending on factors such as the size of the search space (Schwenk et al., 2019b).

[4] https://github.com/facebookresearch/LASER/tree/master/data/tatoeba/v1

Algorithm 1: Doc-level margin-based mining

Given $\mathcal{X}$, $\mathcal{Y}$, k, t, *JOIN_METHOD*
$\mathcal{X}$: Set of sentences in language X. May be grouped into documents or standalone sentences.
$\mathcal{Y}$: Set of sentences in language Y that are parallel or comparable to those in $\mathcal{X}$.
k: Number of neighbors
JOIN_METHOD: Method of combining sentence pairs after mining in the forward and backward directions. One of either INTERSECT or UNION.
t: Margin similarity threshold

MINE SENTENCE PAIRS IN BOTH DIRECTIONS
for *document* $\mathcal{D} \in \mathcal{X}$ **do**
  for $x \in \mathcal{D}$ **do**
    $nn_x \leftarrow NN(x, \mathcal{Y}_\mathcal{D}, k)$;
    // $NN(x, \mathcal{D}, k)$:= Faiss k-nearest neighbors search
    $best_y = \text{argmax}_{y \in nn_x} score(x, y)$;
    // score(x,y) := Eq. (1)
    if $score(x, best_y) > t$ **then**
      $fwd_D \leftarrow (x, best_y)$
    end
    $fwd \leftarrow fwd_D$
  end
end
(Mine in the forward direction)
for $\mathcal{D} \in \mathcal{Y}$ **do**
  for $y \in \mathcal{D}$ **do**
    $nn_y \leftarrow NN(y, \mathcal{X}_\mathcal{D}, k)$
    $best_x = \text{argmax}_{x \in nn_y} score(y, x)$
    if $score(best_x, y) > t$ **then**
      $bwd_D \leftarrow (best_x, y)$
    end
    $bwd \leftarrow bwd_D$
  end
end
(Mine in the backward direction)
if *INTERSECT* **then**
  $\mathcal{P} \leftarrow \{fwd\} \cap \{bwd\}$
end
else if *UNION* **then**
  $\mathcal{P} \leftarrow \{fwd\} \cup \{bwd\}$
end
return $\mathcal{P}$

Algorithm 2: Secondary retrieval procedures

Given $\mathcal{X}, \mathcal{Y}, k, t, \mathcal{M}, JOIN\_METHOD$
t: Margin score threshold
$\mathcal{M}$: An NMT model
if *TRANSLATE* **then**
  if *EN_TO_XX* **then**
    for $x \in \mathcal{X}$ **do**
      $\mathcal{X}_{trans} \leftarrow \mathcal{M}(x \rightarrow lang_y)$
      $\mathcal{P}_{en\_xx} \leftarrow$ *AlgorithmI*$(\mathcal{X}_{trans}, \mathcal{Y}, k, JOIN\_METHOD, t)$
    end
    if not STRICT_INT *or* PAIRWISE_INT **then**
      ; // EN-to-XX trans. only
      return $\mathcal{P}_{en\_xx}$
  end
  if *XX_TO_EN* **then**
    for $y \in \mathcal{Y}$ **do**
      $\mathcal{Y}_{trans} \leftarrow \mathcal{M}(y \rightarrow lang_x)$
      $\mathcal{P}_{xx\_en} \leftarrow$ *AlgorithmI*$(\mathcal{Y}_{trans}, \mathcal{X}, k, JOIN\_METHOD, t)$
    end
    if not STRICT_INT *or* PAIRWISE_INT **then**
      ; // XX-to-EN trans. only
      return $\mathcal{P}_{xx\_en}$
  end
end
$\mathcal{P}_{orig} \leftarrow$ *AlgorithmI*$(\mathcal{X}, \mathcal{Y}, k, JOIN\_METHOD, t)$
; // All-or-nothing voting
if *STRICT_INT* **then**
  return $\mathcal{P}_{orig} \cap \mathcal{P}_{en\_xx} \cap \mathcal{P}_{xx\_en}$
end
; // Majority voting (preferred)
else if *PAIRWISE_INT* **then**
  return $\mathcal{P}_{orig} \cap \mathcal{P}_{en\_xx} \bigcup \mathcal{P}_{orig} \cap \mathcal{P}_{xx\_en} \bigcup \mathcal{P}_{en\_xx} \cap \mathcal{P}_{xx\_en}$
end
; // Vanilla mining
else
  return $\mathcal{P}_{orig}$
end

However, we don't make this hyperparameter a focus of this paper, instead addressing the problem of margin score thresholding and its relation to the size of the search space. We leave a thorough examination of k and its effect on bitext mining performance for future work.

4.2 Filtering Procedures

4.2.1 Thresholding

The most straightforward measure for filtering mined sentence pairs after an initial ("primary") mining pass is to set a similarity score threshold, as shown in Artetxe and Schwenk (2019a). Of course, there is a precision-recall trade-off inherent to adjusting this threshold, and we show that simply using a threshold is problematic in two other ways as well: (1) in the case of document-level mining, the size of the search space (document size) is variable, so a threshold that works well for one document may function poorly for another; and (2) when mining bitexts for NMT training, it can be incredibly expensive to tune this threshold as a hyperparameter, as this entails re-training of the NMT system. Our heuristic method outperforms a previously used margin score threshold (Schwenk et al., 2019b,a; Fan et al., 2020) on document-level mining for Kazakh and Gujarati, doesn't require tuning any hyperparameter, and works for any language for which a supervised MT system is available.

4.2.2 Pre-translation

Our approach capitalizes on multiple similarity-related signals by first translating either the source texts (i.e. en→xx), target texts (xx→en), or both. In our experiments on the Tatoeba dataset (Artetxe and Schwenk, 2019b), we translate with Google

Translate / GNMT (Wu et al., 2016) using Cloud Translation API. However, due to the cost of using this API on large bodies of text, when mining on the English-Kazakh and English-Gujarati comparable corpora, we use an NMT system that we train on WMT'19 data (Barrault et al., 2019), with training corpora sizes given in Table 1. When translating in either direction, we translate the entire corpus, e.g. all English sentences in the Wikipedia corpus are translated to Kazakh.

4.3 Supervised and Unsupervised NMT

We follow the same pipeline for training MT in (Kuwanto et al., 2021) that is based on XLM (Conneau and Lample, 2019). Following their pipeline, we first pretrain a bilingual Language Model (LM) using the Masked Language Model (MLM) objective (Devlin et al., 2019) on the monolingual corpora of two languages (e.g. Kazakh and English for en-kk) obtained from Wikipedia, WMT 2018/2019[5] and Leipzig corpora (2016)[6]. For both the LM pretraining and NMT model fine-tuning, unless otherwise noted, we follow the hyperparameter settings suggested in the XLM repository[7]. For every language pair we extract a shared 60,000 subword vocabulary using Byte-Pair Encoding (BPE) (Sennrich et al., 2016). After pretraining the LM, we train an NMT model in an unsupervised manner following the setup recommended in Conneau and Lample (2019), where both encoder and decoder are initialized using the same pretrained encoder block. For training unsupervised NMT, we use back-translation (*BT*) and denoising auto-encoding (*AE*) losses (Lample et al., 2018a), and the same monolingual data as in LM pretraining. Lastly, to train a supervised MT model using our mined comparable data, we follow *BT+AE* with *BT+MT*, where *MT* stands for supervised machine translation objective for which we use the mined data. We stop training when the validation perplexity (LM pre-training) or BLEU (translation training) was not improved for ten checkpoints. We run all our experiments on 2 GPUs, each with 12GB memory.

We compare the performance in terms of BLEU score of our MT model with a model that follows the same pipeline (LM pre-training, unsupervised MT training, followed by supervised MT training) but that uses gold-standard training data from WMT19 (Table 1). The sizes of the monolingual data we use for LM pretraining are also shown in Table 1.

Train data	Number of sentences	
	en-kk	en-gu
Monolingual	9.51M	1.36M
Supervised		
WMT'19	222,165	22,321
Comparable		
Doc-level mining, threshold = 1.06	430,762	120,989
Doc-level mining with bidirectional pretranslation → majority voting	154,679	113,955

Table 1: Sizes (in number of sentences) of training corpora used in training supervised and semi-supervised NMT. The comparable/pseudoparallel sentences are mined using margin-based scoring with LaBSE with the indicated secondary retrieval procedures. These procedures are described in Section 4.

5 Experiments

5.1 Gold-standard Bitext Retrieval

In gold-standard bitext retrieval tasks, the goal is to mine gold-standard bitexts from a set of parallel or comparable corpora. We use the common approach of finding k-nearest neighbors for each sentence pair (in both directions, if using INTERSECT in Algorithm 1), then choosing the sentence that maximizes the ratio margin score (Equation 1 in Section 4.1).

Tatoeba Dataset[8] The Tatoeba dataset, introduced by Artetxe and Schwenk (2019b), contains up to 1,000 English-aligned, gold-standard sentence pairs for 112 languages. In light of our focus on lower-resource languages, we experiment only on the languages listed in Table 10 of Reimers and Gurevych (2020), which are languages without parallel data for the distillation process they undertake. This heuristic choice is supported by relative performance against languages *with* parallel data for distillation: the average raw cosine similarity baseline with LaBSE for the latter was 96.3, in contrast with 73.7 for the former. Specifically, the ISO 639-2 codes[9] for the languages we use are as follows:

[5] http://data.statmt.org/news-crawl/

[6] https://wortschatz.uni-leipzig.de/en/download/

[7] http://github.com/facebookresearch/XLM

[8] https://github.com/facebookresearch/LASER/tree/master/data/tatoeba/v1

[9] https://www.loc.gov/standards/iso639-2/php/code_list.php

afr, amh, ang, arq, arz, ast, awa, aze, bel, ben, ber, bos, bre, cbk, ceb, cha, cor, csb, cym, dsb, dtp, epo, eus, fao, fry, gla, gle, gsw, hsb, ido, ile, ina, isl, jav, ksb, kaz, khm, kur, kzj, lat, lfn, mal, mhr, nds, nno, nov, oci, orv, pam, pms, swg, swh, tam, tat, tel, tgl tuk, tzl, uig, uzb, war, wuu, xho, yid.

5.2 Pseudo-parallel Sentences From Comparable Corpora

In addition to gold-standard bitext mining, we also mine pseudo-parallel sentences from comparable corpora. The aim of this task is as follows: given two sets of similar documents in different languages, find sentence pairs that are close enough to being translations to act as training data for an NMT system. Of course, unlike the gold-standard mining task, there are not ground-truth labels present for this task, and so evaluation must be performed on a downstream task like NMT.

Comparable Corpora Our comparable data is mined from comparable documents, which are linked Wikipedia pages in different languages obtained using the langlinks from Wikimedia dumps. For each sentence in a foreign language Wikipedia page, we use all sentences in its corresponding linked English language Wikipedia page as potential comparable sentences.

Pre-processing Since our comparable corpora for both EN-KK and EN-GU are grouped into documents, the most important pre-processing step we perform is eliminating especially short documents before similarity search. The motivation for this is that since we search at document-level, the quality of the resulting pairs could be highly degraded in particularly small search spaces, in a way that neither thresholding nor voting could mitigate. Note that average document length was much shorter for both Gujarati and Kazakh than for English, due simply to shorter Wikipedia articles in those languages. For the EN-KK corpus, we omit any paired documents whose English version was < 30 words or whose Kazakh version was < 8 words, which we determine somewhat arbitrarily by seeing what values allowed for a sufficient number of remaining sentences. For the EN-GU corpus, we take a more disciplined approach and lop off the bottom 35% of shortest document pairs, which happened to be $document\_length = 21$ sentences for English and 5 sentences for Gujarati. This step accounted for the large number of documents in each corpus that contained very few sentences.

5.3 NMT Training Data

We conduct experiments on Kazakh and Gujarati. They are spoken by 22M and 55M speakers worldwide, respectively. Additionally, the languages have few parallel but some comparable and/or monolingual data available, which makes them ideal and important candidates for our low-resource unsupervised NMT research.

Our monolingual data for LM pre-training of these languages (shown in Table 1) are carefully chosen from the same topics (for Wikipedia) and the same domain (for news data). For the news data, we also select data from similar time periods (late 2010s) to mitigate domain discrepancy between source and target languages as per previous research (Kim et al., 2020). We also randomly downsample the English part of WMT NewsCrawl corpus so that our English and the corresponding foreign news data are equal in size.

6 Results & Analysis

6.1 Tatoeba Dataset

We mine bitexts on the Tatoeba test set in 64 generally low-resource languages (listed in Section 5.1) using the primary mining procedure described in Algorithm 1 with *intersection* retrieval, in addition to seven different secondary mining procedures, namely:

1. Cosine similarity (Reimers and Gurevych, 2020)
2. Margin scoring with no threshold
3. Margin scoring, threshold=1.06
4. Margin scoring, threshold=1.20 (shown to be optimal on BUCC mining task [10])
5. Margin scoring using EN sentences translated to XX
6. Margin scoring using XX sentences translated to EN
7. The *strict* intersection of pairs generated by methods 2, 5, and 6
8. The *pairwise* intersection of pairs generated by method 2, 5, and 6 (majority voting)

We report F1 instead of accuracy because the intersection methods (in both primary and secondary procedures) permit less than 100% recall.

The results are broken down across languages by resource availability (as in "high-resource" or "low-

[10]https://www.sbert.net/examples/applications/parallel-sentence-mining/README.html

Procedure	Average gain over baseline (best results only)	Average gain over baseline (all results)	Average gain over baseline (langs with transl. support)	Best results by resource capacity*	Average gain over baseline (by resource capacity)
Margin scoring only (Artetxe and Schwenk, 2019a)	**+6.9**	**+5.2**	+3.6	Level 0: 6 lang. Level 1: 18 lang. Level 2: 2 lang. Level 3: 2 lang. 2†, 6‡	Level 0: +7.2 Level 1: **+5.2** Level 2: +1.8 Level 3: +3.4 Level 4: +1.0
xx-to-en translation → margin scoring	+5.2	+3.3	+3.3	Level 0: 1 lang. Level 1: 7 lang. Level 2: 2 lang. Level 3: 7 lang. Level 4: 1 lang.	Level 0: +3.9 Level 1: +2.8 Level 2: +0.1 Level 3: **+4.3** Level 4: **+1.8**
Bidirectional translation → margin scoring → pairwise intersection of three sets of sentence pairs	+4.6	+4.0	**+4.0**	Level 0: 2 lang. Level 1: 3 lang. Level 2: 2 lang. Level 3: 1 lang.	Level 0: **+7.3** Level 1: +3.9 Level 2: **+2.6** Level 3: +4.0 Level 4: +1.0

* Using resource categorizations from Joshi et al. (2020) † Extinct languages ‡ Constructed (artificial) languages

Table 2: Average gain (F1) over the baseline for each mining method on the low-resource subset of the Tatoeba test data, broken down by several categories. The baseline is the F1 achieved using raw cosine similarity with LaBSE. The "best results" for a given method are those results on which that method achieved superior results compared to all other methods. "All results" refers to all languages in the Tatoeba test set.

Corpus	Language pair			
	kk→en	en→kk	gu→en	en→gu
Unsupervised				
Kim et al. (2020)	2.0	0.8	0.6	0.6
Supervised				
WMT'19 (Kim et al., 2020)	10.3	2.4	9.9	3.5
WMT'19 (Tran et al., 2020) Iter 1	9.8	3.4	8.1	8.1
WMT'19 (Tran et al., 2020) Iter 3	**13.2**	4.3	**18.0**	16.9
Google MT (Wu et al., 2016)	**28.9**	**23.1**	**26.2**	**31.4**
Our pipeline: unsup.+sup.				
WMT'19	11.2	7.3	5.7	10.2
Threshold=1.06	6.6	4.1	16.2	19.8
Majority voting	8.6	6.1	16.4	**20.2**
Threshold=1.06+WMT'19	11.8	7.9	15.4	18.5
Majority voting+WMT'19	12.6	**9.0**	15.8	19.1

Table 3: NMT training schemes and corresponding BLEU scores on WMT'19 test set. We train supervised systems with gold-standard data, comparable/pseudoparallel ("silver-standard") data, and combinations of both. We also try supplementing unsupervised training with each of these three types of supervised data. We provide a supervised benchmark from Wu et al. (2016).

resource"), as ranked on a 0-5 scale[11] according to Joshi et al. (2020). These results are summarized in Table 2. We only display results for simple margin scoring (with no threshold), margin scoring with XX-to-EN translation beforehand, and margin scoring with bidirectional pre-translation + majority voting, as these are the best-performing methods for the Tatoeba bitext retrieval task.

Because many of the languages in Table 2 lack support in GNMT, the dominant method overall is simple margin scoring, being the best-performing method on 28/64 languages[12] and seeing an aver-

[11] rb.gy/psmfnz

[12] 6/64 languages lack a resource categorization, so we re-

age gain over the baseline of +5.2 for all languages and +6.9 for languages on which it was the best-performing method. However, for languages with *translation support* (i.e. for which a supervised NMT system is available), the majority voting approach won out, with an average gain over the baseline of +4.0, in contrast to vanilla margin scoring (+3.6). In fact, among these 38 languages, vanilla margin scoring outperformed translation-based or hybrid (intersection) methods on only 11 languages.

Simply translating non-English sentences into English before mining (Method 6) also performed well, netting best results on 18 languages and outperforming other methods on resource level 3 (+4.3 F1 over baseline) and level 4 (+1.8) languages. Meanwhile, pairwise intersection performed best on level 0 (+7.3) and level 2 (+2.6) languages, with vanilla margin scoring outperforming other approaches on level 1 (+5.2).

These results show that the optimal choice of mining approach is very much dependent on the resource availability of the languages involved (most directly, the amount of data available during pre-training), and that if a supervised MT system is already available for a given language, that system can be used for efficient mining of parallel or pseudo-parallel sentences, in tandem with a pre-trained language model like LaBSE. As shown in Table 2, even high-resource (i.e. level 4) languages can be helped by pre-translation of paired corpora.

6.2 NMT

In Table 3, we show the performance in terms of BLEU scores of various NMT training schemes on the same WMT'19 test set. We train the supervised MT part of our pipeline system with gold-standard (WMT'19) data, our mined comparable/pseudoparallel ("silver-standard") data, and combinations of both i.e., training with comparable data followed by training with gold-standard data. We also provide Google massively multilingual MT performance on the same WMT'19 test set (Wu et al., 2016).

As can be seen in Table 3, our method of mining bitext without thresholding results in higher BLEU performance than when using bitexts mined using margin scoring with a threshold of 1.06, which is a commonly used threshold recommended by previous works for margin-based mining (Schwenk et al., 2019b,a). Our preferred method also results in the best en→gu performance, which outperforms previous unsupervised or supervised works. It outperforms the best previous work that uses WMT'19 data and iterative bitext mining by +3.3 BLEU. Since we do not perform iterative mining, if we consider the same previous work without iterative mining i.e., Tran et al. (2020) Iter 1, our approach outperforms that model by +12.1 BLEU in en→gu direction and by +8.3 BLEU in gu→en direction.

When combined with supervised i.e., gold-standard, data for training, our method for mining bitext which does not use any thresholding (majority voting+WMT'19) also outperforms the same model which uses bitext mined using margin scoring with a threshold of 1.06 (Threshold=1.06+WMT'19). Majority voting+WMT'19 also results in the best en→kk performance, which outperforms previous unsupervised or supervised works. It outperforms the best previous work that uses WMT'19 data and iterative bitext mining by +4.7 BLEU. Since we do not perform iterative mining, if we consider the same previous work without iterative mining i.e., Tran et al. (2020) Iter 1, our approach outperforms that model by +5.6 BLEU in the en→kk direction and by +2.8 BLEU in the kk→en direction. It is also worth noting that for training our pipeline model we use the default hyperparameter settings suggested in the XLM repository, while previous works perform extensive hyperparameter tuning. We believe our performance can be improved further by tuning our hyperparameter settings, but for brevity leave this for a future study. These results on low resource MT further demonstrate the superiority of our method for mining bitext without thresholding—compared to margin scoring *with* thresholding—for downstream low-resource MT applications. To our knowledge, we are the first to thoroughly investigate secondary filtering methods for selecting bitexts following a primary, similarity-based mining procedure.

7 Conclusion

We propose a novel method of mining sentence pairs from both comparable and parallel corpora, and demonstrate success on both the Tatoeba gold-standard similarity search task and on mining pseudo-parallel sentences for downstream NMT training. We uncover the problematic nature of setting a similarity score threshold for this task, particularly in the context of document-level min-

port results on the remaining 58

ing. We introduce a heuristic algorithm that filters translations from non-translations by voting on sentence pairs mined in three different ways, which avoids having to laboriously train and re-train NMT systems to tune a similarity score threshold.

References

Waleed Ammar, George Mulcaire, Yulia Tsvetkov, Guillaume Lample, Chris Dyer, and Noah A. Smith. 2016. Massively Multilingual Word Embeddings. *arXiv e-prints, arXiv:1602.01925*.

Sanjeev Arora, Yingyu Liang, and Tengyu Ma. 2017. A Simple but Tough-to-Beat Baseline for Sentence Embeddings. *International Conference on Learning Representations 2017*.

Mikel Artetxe, Gorka Labaka, and Eneko Agirre. 2018a. Unsupervised Statistical Machine Translation. In *Proceedings of the 2018 Conference on Empirical Methods in Natural Language Processing*, pages 3632–3642, Brussels, Belgium. Association for Computational Linguistics.

Mikel Artetxe, Gorka Labaka, and Eneko Agirre. 2019a. An Effective Approach to Unsupervised Machine Translation. In *Proceedings of the 57th Annual Meeting of the Association for Computational Linguistics*, pages 194–203, Florence, Italy. Association for Computational Linguistics.

Mikel Artetxe, Gorka Labaka, and Eneko Agirre. 2019b. Bilingual Lexicon Induction through Unsupervised Machine Translation. In *Proceedings of the 57th Annual Meeting of the Association for Computational Linguistics*, pages 5002–5007, Florence, Italy. Association for Computational Linguistics.

Mikel Artetxe, Gorka Labaka, Eneko Agirre, and Kyunghyun Cho. 2018b. Unsupervised Neural Machine Translation. In *International Conference on Learning Representations 2018*.

Mikel Artetxe and Holger Schwenk. 2019a. Margin-based parallel corpus mining with multilingual sentence embeddings. In *Proceedings of the 57th Annual Meeting of the Association for Computational Linguistics*, pages 3197–3203, Florence, Italy. Association for Computational Linguistics.

Mikel Artetxe and Holger Schwenk. 2019b. Massively Multilingual Sentence Embeddings for Zero-Shot Cross-Lingual Transfer and Beyond. *Transactions of the Association for Computational Linguistics*, 7:597–610.

Adoni Azpeitia, Thierry Etchegoyhen, and Eva Martinez Garcia. 2018. Extracting Parallel Sentences from Comparable Corpora with STACC Variants. In *Proceedings of the Eleventh International Conference on Language Resources and Evaluation (LREC 2018)*, Paris, France. European Language Resources Association (ELRA).

Andoni Azpeitia, Thierry Etchegoyhen, and Eva Martínez Garcia. 2017. Weighted set-theoretic alignment of comparable sentences. In *Proceedings of the 10th Workshop on Building and Using Comparable Corpora*, pages 41–45, Vancouver, Canada. Association for Computational Linguistics.

Loïc Barrault, Ondřej Bojar, Marta R. Costa-jussà, Christian Federmann, Mark Fishel, Yvette Graham, Barry Haddow, Matthias Huck, Philipp Koehn, Shervin Malmasi, Christof Monz, Mathias Müller, Santanu Pal, Matt Post, and Marcos Zampieri. 2019. Findings of the 2019 conference on machine translation (WMT19). In *Proceedings of the Fourth Conference on Machine Translation (Volume 2: Shared Task Papers, Day 1)*, pages 1–61, Florence, Italy. Association for Computational Linguistics.

Houda Bouamor and Hassan Sajjad. 2018. H2@BUCC18: Parallel Sentence Extraction from Comparable Corpora Using Multilingual Sentence Embeddings. In *Proceedings of the Eleventh International Conference on Language Resources and Evaluation (LREC 2018)*, Paris, France. European Language Resources Association (ELRA).

Alexis Conneau, Kartikay Khandelwal, Naman Goyal, Vishrav Chaudhary, Guillaume Wenzek, Francisco Guzmán, Edouard Grave, Myle Ott, Luke Zettlemoyer, and Veselin Stoyanov. 2020. Unsupervised cross-lingual representation learning at scale. In *Proceedings of the 58th Annual Meeting of the Association for Computational Linguistics*, pages 8440–8451, Online. Association for Computational Linguistics.

Alexis Conneau, Douwe Kiela, Holger Schwenk, Loic Barrault, and Antoine Bordes. 2017. Supervised Learning of Universal Sentence Representations from Natural Language Inference Data. *arXiv e-prints*, page arXiv:1705.02364.

Alexis Conneau and Guillaume Lample. 2019. Cross-lingual Language Model Pretraining. In *Advances in Neural Information Processing Systems*, volume 32. Curran Associates, Inc.

Jacob Devlin, Ming-Wei Chang, Kenton Lee, and Kristina Toutanova. 2019. BERT: Pre-training of deep bidirectional transformers for language understanding. In *Proceedings of the 2019 Conference of the North American Chapter of the Association for Computational Linguistics: Human Language Technologies, Volume 1 (Long and Short Papers)*, pages 4171–4186, Minneapolis, Minnesota. Association for Computational Linguistics.

Georgiana Dinu, Angeliki Lazaridou, and Marco Baroni. 2014. Improving Zero-shot Learning by Mitigating the Hubness Problem. *arXiv e-prints*, page arXiv:1412.6568.

Angela Fan, Shruti Bhosale, Holger Schwenk, Zhiyi Ma, Ahmed El-Kishky, Siddharth Goyal, Mandeep Baines, Onur Celebi, Guillaume Wenzek,

Vishrav Chaudhary, Naman Goyal, Tom Birch, Vitaliy Liptchinsky, Sergey Edunov, Edouard Grave, Michael Auli, and Armand Joulin. 2020. Beyond English-Centric Multilingual Machine Translation. *arXiv e-prints*, page arXiv:2010.11125.

Fangxiaoyu Feng, Yinfei Yang, Daniel Cer, Naveen Arivazhagan, and Wei Wang. 2020. Language-agnostic BERT Sentence Embedding. *arXiv e-prints*, page arXiv:2007.01852.

Pascale Fung and Percy Cheung. 2004. Multi-level bootstrapping for extracting parallel sentences from a quasi-comparable corpus. In *COLING 2004: Proceedings of the 20th International Conference on Computational Linguistics*, pages 1051–1057, Geneva, Switzerland. COLING.

Viktor Hangya, Fabienne Braune, Yuliya Kalasouskaya, and Alexander Fraser. 2018. Unsupervised Parallel Sentence Extraction from Comparable Corpora. In *Proceedings of the 15th International Workshop on Spoken Language Translation*, pages 7–13, Bruges, Belgium.

Viktor Hangya and Alexander Fraser. 2019. Unsupervised parallel sentence extraction with parallel segment detection helps machine translation. In *Proceedings of the 57th Annual Meeting of the Association for Computational Linguistics*, pages 1224–1234, Florence, Italy. Association for Computational Linguistics.

Vu Cong Duy Hoang, Philipp Koehn, Gholamreza Haffari, and Trevor Cohn. 2018. Iterative back-translation for neural machine translation. In *Proceedings of the 2nd Workshop on Neural Machine Translation and Generation*, pages 18–24, Melbourne, Australia. Association for Computational Linguistics.

Jeff Johnson, Matthijs Douze, and Hervé Jégou. 2017. Billion-scale Similarity Search with GPUs. *arXiv e-prints*, page arXiv:1702.08734.

Pratik Joshi, Sebastin Santy, Amar Budhiraja, Kalika Bali, and Monojit Choudhury. 2020. The state and fate of linguistic diversity and inclusion in the NLP world. In *Proceedings of the 58th Annual Meeting of the Association for Computational Linguistics*, pages 6282–6293, Online. Association for Computational Linguistics.

Phillip Keung, Julian Salazar, Yichao Lu, and Noah A. Smith. 2020. Unsupervised bitext mining and translation via self-trained contextual embeddings. *Transactions of the Association for Computational Linguistics*, 8:828–841.

Yunsu Kim, Miguel Graça, and Hermann Ney. 2020. When and why is unsupervised neural machine translation useless? In *Proceedings of the 22nd Annual Conference of the European Association for Machine Translation*, pages 35–44, Lisboa, Portugal. European Association for Machine Translation.

Ryan Kiros, Yukun Zhu, Ruslan Salakhutdinov, Richard S. Zemel, Antonio Torralba, Raquel Urtasun, and Sanja Fidler. 2015. Skip-Thought Vectors. *arXiv e-prints*, page arXiv:1506.06726.

Alexandre Klementiev, Ivan Titov, and Binod Bhattarai. 2012. Inducing crosslingual distributed representations of words. In *Proceedings of COLING 2012*, pages 1459–1474, Mumbai, India. The COLING 2012 Organizing Committee.

Garry Kuwanto, Afra Feyza Akyürek, Isidora Chara Tourni, Siyang Li, and Derry Wijaya. 2021. Low-Resource Machine Translation for Low-Resource Languages: Leveraging Comparable Data, Code-Switching and Compute Resources. *arXiv preprint arXiv:2103.13272.*

Ivana Kvapilíková, Mikel Artetxe, Gorka Labaka, Eneko Agirre, and Ondřej Bojar. 2020. Unsupervised multilingual sentence embeddings for parallel corpus mining. In *Proceedings of the 58th Annual Meeting of the Association for Computational Linguistics: Student Research Workshop*, pages 255–262, Online. Association for Computational Linguistics.

Guillaume Lample, Alexis Conneau, Ludovic Denoyer, and Marc'Aurelio Ranzato. 2017. Unsupervised Machine Translation Using Monolingual Corpora Only. *arXiv preprint arXiv:1711.00043.*

Guillaume Lample, Alexis Conneau, Ludovic Denoyer, and Marc'Aurelio Ranzato. 2018a. Unsupervised machine translation using monolingual corpora only. In *International Conference on Learning Representations.*

Guillaume Lample, Alexis Conneau, Marc'Aurelio Ranzato, Ludovic Denoyer, and Hervé Jégou. 2018b. Word translation without parallel data. In *International Conference on Learning Representations.*

Guillaume Lample, Myle Ott, Alexis Conneau, Ludovic Denoyer, and Marc'Aurelio Ranzato. 2018c. Phrase-based & neural unsupervised machine translation. In *Proceedings of the 2018 Conference on Empirical Methods in Natural Language Processing*, pages 5039–5049, Brussels, Belgium. Association for Computational Linguistics.

Yinhan Liu, Myle Ott, Naman Goyal, Jingfei Du, Mandar Joshi, Danqi Chen, Omer Levy, Mike Lewis, Luke Zettlemoyer, and Veselin Stoyanov. 2019. RoBERTa: A Robustly Optimized BERT Pretraining Approach. *arXiv e-prints*, page arXiv:1907.11692.

Kelly Marchisio, Kevin Duh, and Philipp Koehn. 2020. When does unsupervised machine translation work? In *Proceedings of the Fifth Conference on Machine Translation*, pages 571–583, Online. Association for Computational Linguistics.

Tomas Mikolov, Ilya Sutskever, Kai Chen, Greg Corrado, and Jeffrey Dean. 2013. Distributed Representations of Words and Phrases and Their Compositionality. In *Proceedings of the 26th International Conference on Neural Information Processing Systems - Volume 2*, NIPS'13, page 3111–3119, Red Hook, NY, USA. Curran Associates Inc.

Dragos Stefan Munteanu, Alexander Fraser, and Daniel Marcu. 2004. Improved machine translation performance via parallel sentence extraction from comparable corpora. In *Proceedings of the Human Language Technology Conference of the North American Chapter of the Association for Computational Linguistics: HLT-NAACL 2004*, pages 265–272, Boston, Massachusetts, USA. Association for Computational Linguistics.

Dragos Stefan Munteanu and Daniel Marcu. 2006. Extracting parallel sub-sentential fragments from non-parallel corpora. In *Proceedings of the 21st International Conference on Computational Linguistics and 44th Annual Meeting of the Association for Computational Linguistics*, pages 81–88, Sydney, Australia. Association for Computational Linguistics.

Jeffrey Pennington, Richard Socher, and Christopher Manning. 2014. GloVe: Global vectors for word representation. In *Proceedings of the 2014 Conference on Empirical Methods in Natural Language Processing (EMNLP)*, pages 1532–1543, Doha, Qatar. Association for Computational Linguistics.

Matthew Peters, Mark Neumann, Mohit Iyyer, Matt Gardner, Christopher Clark, Kenton Lee, and Luke Zettlemoyer. 2018. Deep contextualized word representations. In *Proceedings of the 2018 Conference of the North American Chapter of the Association for Computational Linguistics: Human Language Technologies, Volume 1 (Long Papers)*, pages 2227–2237, New Orleans, Louisiana. Association for Computational Linguistics.

Nima Pourdamghani, Nada Aldarrab, Marjan Ghazvininejad, Kevin Knight, and Jonathan May. 2019. Translating translationese: A two-step approach to unsupervised machine translation. In *Proceedings of the 57th Annual Meeting of the Association for Computational Linguistics*, pages 3057–3062, Florence, Italy. Association for Computational Linguistics.

Sree Harsha Ramesh and Krishna Prasad Sankaranarayanan. 2018. Neural machine translation for low resource languages using bilingual lexicon induced from comparable corpora. In *Proceedings of the 2018 Conference of the North American Chapter of the Association for Computational Linguistics: Student Research Workshop*, pages 112–119, New Orleans, Louisiana, USA. Association for Computational Linguistics.

Nils Reimers and Iryna Gurevych. 2019. Sentence-BERT: Sentence embeddings using Siamese BERT-networks. In *Proceedings of the 2019 Conference on Empirical Methods in Natural Language Processing and the 9th International Joint Conference on Natural Language Processing (EMNLP-IJCNLP)*, pages 3982–3992, Hong Kong, China. Association for Computational Linguistics.

Nils Reimers and Iryna Gurevych. 2020. Making monolingual sentence embeddings multilingual using knowledge distillation. In *Proceedings of the 2020 Conference on Empirical Methods in Natural Language Processing (EMNLP)*, pages 4512–4525, Online. Association for Computational Linguistics.

Philip Resnik and Noah A. Smith. 2003. The web as a parallel corpus. *Computational Linguistics*, 29(3):349–380.

Holger Schwenk. 2018. Filtering and mining parallel data in a joint multilingual space. In *Proceedings of the 56th Annual Meeting of the Association for Computational Linguistics (Volume 2: Short Papers)*, pages 228–234, Melbourne, Australia. Association for Computational Linguistics.

Holger Schwenk, Vishrav Chaudhary, Shuo Sun, Hongyu Gong, and Francisco Guzmán. 2019a. WikiMatrix: Mining 135M Parallel Sentences in 1620 Language Pairs from Wikipedia. *arXiv e-prints*, page arXiv:1907.05791.

Holger Schwenk and Matthijs Douze. 2017. Learning joint multilingual sentence representations with neural machine translation. In *Proceedings of the 2nd Workshop on Representation Learning for NLP*, pages 157–167, Vancouver, Canada. Association for Computational Linguistics.

Holger Schwenk, Guillaume Wenzek, Sergey Edunov, Edouard Grave, and Armand Joulin. 2019b. CCMatrix: Mining Billions of High-Quality Parallel Sentences on the WEB. *arXiv e-prints*, page arXiv:1911.04944.

Rico Sennrich, Barry Haddow, and Alexandra Birch. 2016. Neural machine translation of rare words with subword units. In *Proceedings of the 54th Annual Meeting of the Association for Computational Linguistics (Volume 1: Long Papers)*, pages 1715–1725, Berlin, Germany. Association for Computational Linguistics.

Kaitao Song, Xu Tan, Tao Qin, Jianfeng Lu, and Tie-Yan Liu. 2019. MASS: Masked Sequence to Sequence Pre-training for Language Generation. *arXiv e-prints*, page arXiv:1905.02450.

Sandeep Subramanian, Adam Trischler, Yoshua Bengio, and Christopher J Pal. 2018. Learning General Purpose Distributed Sentence Representations via Large Scale Multi-task Learning. *arXiv e-prints*, page arXiv:1804.00079.

Chau Tran, Yuqing Tang, Xian Li, and Jiatao Gu. 2020. Cross-lingual Retrieval for Iterative Self-Supervised Training. *arXiv e-prints*, page arXiv:2006.09526.

Zirui Wang, Jiateng Xie, Ruochen Xu, Yiming Yang, Graham Neubig, and Jaime Carbonell. 2019. Cross-lingual Alignment vs Joint Training: A Comparative Study and A Simple Unified Framework. *arXiv e-prints*, page arXiv:1910.04708.

Lijun Wu, Jinhua Zhu, Di He, Fei Gao, Tao Qin, Jianhuang Lai, and Tie-Yan Liu. 2019. Machine translation with weakly paired documents. In *Proceedings of the 2019 Conference on Empirical Methods in Natural Language Processing and the 9th International Joint Conference on Natural Language Processing (EMNLP-IJCNLP)*, pages 4375–4384, Hong Kong, China. Association for Computational Linguistics.

Yonghui Wu, Mike Schuster, Zhifeng Chen, Quoc V. Le, Mohammad Norouzi, Wolfgang Macherey, Maxim Krikun, Yuan Cao, Qin Gao, Klaus Macherey, Jeff Klingner, Apurva Shah, Melvin Johnson, Xiaobing Liu, Łukasz Kaiser, Stephan Gouws, Yoshikiyo Kato, Taku Kudo, Hideto Kazawa, Keith Stevens, George Kurian, Nishant Patil, Wei Wang, Cliff Young, Jason Smith, Jason Riesa, Alex Rudnick, Oriol Vinyals, Greg Corrado, Macduff Hughes, and Jeffrey Dean. 2016. Google's Neural Machine Translation System: Bridging the Gap between Human and Machine Translation. *arXiv e-prints*, page arXiv:1609.08144.

Bing Zhao and Stephan Vogel. 2002. Adaptive Parallel Sentences Mining from Web Bilingual News Collection. In *Proceedings of the 2002 IEEE International Conference on Data Mining*, ICDM '02, page 745, USA. IEEE Computer Society.

Pierre Zweigenbaum, Serge Sharoff, and Reinhard Rapp. 2017. Overview of the second BUCC shared task: Spotting parallel sentences in comparable corpora. In *Proceedings of the 10th Workshop on Building and Using Comparable Corpora*, pages 60–67, Vancouver, Canada. Association for Computational Linguistics.

Pierre Zweigenbaum, Serge Sharoff, and Reinhard Rapp. 2018. Overview of the Third BUCC Shared Task: Spotting Parallel Sentences in Comparable Corpora. In *Workshop on Building and Using Comparable Corpora*, Miyazaki, Japan.

A Appendix

Procedure	afr	amh	ang	arq	arz	ast	awa	aze	bel	ben	ber	bos	bre
Raw cosine similarity (*Acc=F1*)	97.4	94	64.2	46.2	78.4	90.6	73.2	96.1	96.2	91.3	10.4	96.2	17.3
Margin scoring, *intersection*, no threshold (*F1*)	98.7	94.2	**73.4**	**57.2**	**84.6**	**94.3**	**83.4**	97.4	97.5	92.4	**14.2**	96.6	**21.5**
Precision	*99.9*	*96.9*	*88.4*	*80.0*	*93.6*	*98.3*	*95.5*	*99.3*	*99.1*	*96.6*	*30.9*	*98.0*	*38.5*
Recall	*97.6*	*91.7*	*62.7*	*44.5*	*77.1*	*90.6*	*74.0*	*95.6*	*95.9*	*88.5*	*9.2*	*95.2*	*14.9*
Margin scoring, *intersection*, threshold = 1.06 (*F1*)	98.2	94.5	72.9	56.0	84.0	94.2	80.5	97.2	97.3	91.8	13.4	96.4	21.3
Precision	*100*	*97.5*	*90.1*	*85.0*	*95.7*	*99.1*	*97.0*	*99.3*	*99.1*	*96.9*	*44.4*	*98.0*	*54.1*
Recall	*96.5*	*91.7*	*61.2*	*41.7*	*74.8*	*89.8*	*68.8*	*95.3*	*95.6*	*87.3*	*7.9*	*94.9*	*13.3*
Margin scoring, *intersection*, threshold = 1.20 (*F1*)	89.5	82.5	59.1	43.6	76.9	92.4	57.2	89.6	94.8	78.6	11.8	90.5	13.4
Precision	*100*	*100*	*96.6*	*97.3*	*98.1*	*99.1*	*98.9*	*99.8*	*99.5*	*99.1*	*90.0*	*99.0*	*92.3*
Recall	*81.0*	*70.2*	*42.5*	*28.1*	*63.3*	*86.6*	*40.3*	*81.4*	*90.5*	*65.1*	*6.3*	*83.3*	*7.2*
Margin scoring, *intersection*, en-xx (*F1*)	98.4	93.2	*	*	*	*	*	96.7	97.6	91.8	*	96.3	*
Precision	*99.6*	*96.8*	*	*	*	*	*	*98.6*	*99.1*	*96.5*	*	*98.2*	*
Recall	*97.3*	*89.9*	*	*	*	*	*	*94.9*	*96.1*	*87.6*	*	*94.4*	*
Margin scoring, *intersection*, xx-en (*F1*)	**99.0**	**95.7**	*	*	*	*	*	**97.6**	97.6	92.0	*	97.3	*
Precision	*99.8*	*98.1*	*	*	*	*	*	*99.0*	*99.1*	*96.3*	*	*98.8*	*
Recall	*98.2*	*93.5*	*	*	*	*	*	*96.3*	*96.1*	*88.0*	*	*95.8*	*
Margin scoring, *intersection*, strict intersection (*F1*)	98.1	93.7	*	*	*	*	*	96.2	96.9	89.8	*	96.0	*
Precision	*100*	*100*	*	*	*	*	*	*99.8*	*99.8*	*99.3*	*	*100*	*
Recall	*96.2*	*88.1*	*	*	*	*	*	*92.8*	*94.2*	*82.0*	*	*92.4*	*
Margin scoring, *intersection*, majority vote (*F1*)	98.9	95.4	*	*	*	*	*	97.5	**97.9**	**93.0**	*	97.1	*
Precision	*99.9*	*98.7*	*	*	*	*	*	*99.3*	*99.6*	*97.9*	*	*98.8*	*
Recall	*97.9*	*92.3*	*	*	*	*	*	*95.9*	*96.2*	*88.6*	*	*95.5*	*

Procedure	cbk	ceb	cha	cor	csb	cym	dsb	dtp	epo	eus	fao	fry	gla
Raw cosine similarity (*Acc=F1*)	82.5	70.9	39.8	12.8	56.1	93.6	69.3	13.3	98.4	95.8	90.6	89.9	88.8
Margin scoring, *intersection*, no threshold (*F1*)	**89.5**	79.3	**49.3**	**18.8**	**69.5**	96.2	**80.7**	**18.8**	**99.0**	96.8	**94.9**	93.7	91.9
Precision	*96.7*	*91.1*	*65.9*	*45.2*	*86.5*	*98.9*	*94.7*	*37.5*	*99.7*	*98.4*	*98.0*	*96.9*	*97.1*
Recall	*83.2*	*70.2*	*39.4*	*11.9*	*58.1*	*93.6*	*70.4*	*12.5*	*98.4*	*95.2*	*92.0*	*90.8*	*87.3*
Margin scoring, *intersection*, threshold = 1.06 (*F1*)	87.1	78.5	47.8	16.2	68.0	95.6	79.1	18.5	99.0	96.4	93.4	93.1	91.2
Precision	*97.8*	*93.3*	*75.0*	*64.1*	*90.2*	*99.1*	*95.6*	*56.1*	*99.9*	*98.5*	*98.7*	*97.5*	*97.3*
Recall	*78.6*	*67.7*	*35.0*	*9.3*	*54.5*	*92.3*	*67.4*	*11.1*	*98.2*	*94.4*	*88.5*	*89.0*	*85.8*
Margin scoring, *intersection*, threshold = 1.20 (*F1*)	71.5	67.4	44.3	9.0	54.2	86.0	93.4	15.2	97.9	92.6	84.5	89.5	80.3
Precision	*99.6*	*98.7*	*85.4*	*100*	*95..0*	*99.3*	*99.6*	*87.4*	*99.9*	*99.2*	*99.0*	*99.3*	*98.9*
Recall	*55.7*	*51.2*	*29.9*	*4.7*	*37.9*	*75.8*	*46.6*	*8.3*	*96.0*	*86.8*	*73.7*	*81.5*	*67.6*
Margin scoring, *intersection*, en-xx (*F1*)	*	78.6	*	15.0	*	96.3	76.2	*	98.5	96.4	*	**96.4**	92.6
Precision	*	*90.6*	*	*36.0*	*	*98.9*	*95.0*	*	*99.5*	*98.6*	*	*98.8*	*97.1*
Recall	*	*69.3*	*	*9.5*	*	*93.9*	*63.7*	*	*97.6*	*94.3*	*	*94.2*	*88.4*
Margin scoring, *intersection*, xx-en (*F1*)	*	**86.1**	*	17.3	*	**97.3**	67.3	*	98.9	**97.6**	*	95.6	**93.9**
Precision	*	*94.2*	*	*41.8*	*	*98.9*	*85.5*	*	*99.6*	*98.8*	*	*97.6*	*97.5*
Recall	*	*79.2*	*	*10.9*	*	*95.7*	*55.5*	*	*98.3*	*96.4*	*	*93.6*	*90.6*
Margin scoring, *intersection*, strict intersection (*F1*)	*	77.3	*	13.0	*	95.2	63.0	*	98.5	96.2	*	93.9	89.9
Precision	*	*99.2*	*	*68.6*	*	*100*	*99.1*	*	*100*	*99.5*	*	*98.7*	*99.3*
Recall	*	*63.3*	*	*7.2*	*	*90.8*	*46.1*	*	*97.1*	*93.1*	*	*89.6*	*82.1*
Margin scoring, *intersection*, majority vote (*F1*)	*	81.8	*	18.7	*	96.7	79.4	*	98.8	96.8	*	95.8	93.5
Precision	*	*96.0*	*	*47.9*	*	*99.1*	*97.3*	*	*99.6*	*98.6*	*	*98.8*	*98.0*
Recall	*	*71.3*	*	*11.6*	*	*94.4*	*67.0*	*	*98.1*	*95.2*	*	*93.1*	*89.4*

Procedure	gle	gsw	hsb	ido	ile	ina	isl	jav	kab	kaz	khm	kur	kzj
Raw cosine similarity (*Acc=F1*)	95.0	52.1	71.2	90.9	87.1	95.8	96.2	84.4	6.2	90.5	83.2	87.1	14.2
Margin scoring, *intersection*, no threshold (*F1*)	96.6	62.0	81.6	**95.1**	**93.0**	**97.4**	**97.9**	**92.2**	**7.7**	92.6	86.8	92.1	**20.8**
Precision	*98.7*	*85.1*	*94.6*	*98.7*	*98.4*	*99.0*	*99.4*	*98.9*	*19.4*	*96.8*	*93.0*	*98.1*	*41.3*
Recall	*94.6*	*48.7*	*71.8*	*91.7*	*88.1*	*95.9*	*96.4*	*86.3*	*4.8*	*88.7*	*81.3*	*86.8*	*13.9*
Margin scoring, *intersection*, threshold = 1.06 (*F1*)	95.9	60.2	79.7	94.1	91.7	96.9	97.5	91.6	7.3	92.2	86.4	91.4	20.0
Precision	*98.9*	*89.8*	*94.9*	*99.0*	*99.0*	*99.0*	*99.4*	*99.4*	*31.3*	*96.9*	*94.7*	*98.3*	*55.2*
Recall	*93.1*	*45.3*	*68.7*	*89.7*	*85.4*	*95.0*	*95.7*	*84.9*	*4.1*	*87.8*	*79.5*	*85.4*	*12.2*
Margin scoring, *intersection*, threshold = 1.20 (*F1*)	84.7	43.7	67.8	88.5	77.9	94.5	91.0	83.6	5.0	85.7	76.4	82.9	15.1
Precision	*100*	*97.1*	*99.6*	*99.9*	*99.8*	*99.4*	*99.9*	*99.3*	*78.8*	*99.1*	*98.7*	*99.7*	*94.3*
Recall	*73.5*	*28.2*	*51.3*	*79.5*	*63.8*	*90.0*	*83.6*	*72.2*	*2.6*	*75.5*	*62.3*	*71.0*	*8.2*
Margin scoring, *intersection*, en-xx (*F1*)	96.9	58.7	76.6	80.4	76.4	96.3	91.9	*	*	92.6	87.3	92.0	*
Precision	*98.8*	*80.6*	*92.9*	*91.8*	*90.1*	*99.4*	*96.4*	*	*	*97.0*	*93.9*	*97.5*	*

Recall	95.2	46.2	65.2	71.6	66.3	93.5	87.8	*	*	88.7	81.6	97.1	*
Margin scoring, *intersection*, xx-en (*F1*)	97.7	59.3	80.0	82.1	78.7	95.8	80.8	*	*	**93.5**	87.5	**95.6**	*
Precision	99.0	83.1	93.1	95.4	93.0	98.6	93.8	*	*	96.8	93.5	99.2	*
Recall	96.4	46.2	70.2	72.0	68.2	93.2	71.0	*	*	90.4	82.1	92.2	*
Margin scoring, *intersection*, strict intersection (*F1*)	95.6	55.1	74.7	73.2	67.0	94.9	78.2	*	*	91.2	85.6	90.3	*
Precision	99.6	91.2	96.1	100	99.8	99.7	99.8	*	*	99.2	98.2	99.4	*
Recall	92.0	39.3	61.2	57.7	50.4	90.6	64.3	*	*	84.3	75.9	82.7	*
Margin scoring, *intersection*, majority vote (*F1*)	**97.8**	**62.3**	**81.7**	91.1	88.4	97.1	96.6	*	*	93.1	**87.8**	94.0	*
Precision	99.3	86.4	94.8	99.5	99.3	99.1	99.3	*	*	97.5	94.9	99.2	*
Recall	73.5	28.2	51.3	79.5	63.8	90.0	83.6	72.2	2.6	75.5	62.3	71.0	8.2
Procedure	**lat**	**lfn**	**mal**	**mhr**	**nds**	**nno**	**nov**	**oci**	**orv**	**pam**	**pms**	**swg**	**swh**
Raw cosine similarity (*Acc=F1*)	82.0	71.2	98.9	19.2	81.2	95.9	78.2	69.9	46.8	13.6	67.0	65.2	88.6
Margin scoring, *intersection*, no threshold (*F1*)	**89.0**	**80.7**	**99.3***	26.3	**89.0**	97.5	**85.4**	**78.7**	**57.4**	**17.9**	**78.9**	**80.4**	93.2
Precision	96.8	93.4	99.7	46.0	96.9	99.4	93.5	90.6	78.6	34.6	92.8	95.1	97.7
Recall	82.4	71.0	98.8	18.4	82.2	95.7	78.6	69.6	45.3	12.1	68.6	69.6	89.0
Margin scoring, *intersection*, threshold = 1.06 (*F1*)	87.2	79.4	**99.3***	**26.3**	87.6	97.2	83.0	77.7	55.9	17.4	76.3	77.0	92.5
Precision	97.6	94.7	99.7	59.3	98.3	99.5	94.5	93.1	83.6	50.2	94.4	96.0	98.8
Recall	78.7	68.4	98.8	16.9	79.1	95.1	73.9	66.6	42.0	10.5	64.0	64.3	86.9
Margin scoring, *intersection*, threshold = 1.20 (*F1*)	72.6	68.8	96.4	18.0	74.8	92.1	77.3	65.8	37.0	11.7	63.0	72.3	81.8
Precision	99.5	98.5	99.7	90.1	99.3	99.9	98.8	98.8	96.5	85.1	98.4	98.5	100
Recall	57.2	52.9	93.3	10.0	60.0	85.5	63.4	49.3	22.9	6.3	46.3	57.1	69.2
Margin scoring, *intersection*, en-xx (*F1*)	83.5	*	98.0	*	86.0	97.3	*	*	*	*	*	*	94.9
Precision	95.1	*	99.5	*	97.5	99.3	*	*	*	*	*	*	98.6
Recall	74.4	*	96.5	*	76.9	95.4	*	*	*	*	*	*	91.5
Margin scoring, *intersection*, xx-en (*F1*)	86.1	*	98.2	*	83.8	97.7	*	*	*	*	*	*	95.3
Precision	95.6	*	99.6	*	95.2	99.4	*	*	*	*	*	*	98.1
Recall	78.3	*	96.9	*	74.9	96.1	*	*	*	*	*	*	92.6
Margin scoring, *intersection*, strict intersection (*F1*)	81.7	*	97.1	*	80.1	96.6	*	*	*	*	*	*	92.1
Precision	98.2	*	100	*	99.3	99.8	*	*	*	*	*	*	100
Recall	69.9	*	94.3	*	67.2	93.7	*	*	*	*	*	*	85.4
Margin scoring, *intersection*, majority vote (*F1*)	88.8	*	99.2	*	88.4	**97.8**	*	*	*	*	*	*	**95.5**
Precision	97.1	*	99.9	*	98.3	99.6	*	*	*	*	*	*	99.4
Recall	81.7	*	98.5	*	80.4	96.0	*	*	*	*	*	*	91.2
Procedure	**tam**	**tat**	**tel**	**tgl**	**tuk**	**tzl**	**uig**	**uzb**	**war**	**wuu**	**xho**	**yid**	
Raw cosine similarity (*Acc=F1*)	90.7	87.9	98.3	97.4	80.0	63.0	93.7	86.8	65.3	90.3	91.9	91.0	*
Margin scoring, *intersection*, no threshold (*F1*)	93.0	92.0	**99.1***	98.6	86.8	**71.0**	95.4	91.1	**75.8**	**94.8**	94.2	95.2	*
Precision	97.5	97.4	99.6	99.7	95.8	82.3	98.3	96.8	89.5	98.8	97.7	98.7	*
Recall	88.9	87.1	98.7	97.6	79.3	62.5	92.7	86.0	65.7	91.1	90.8	92.0	*
Margin scoring, *intersection*, threshold = 1.06 (*F1*)	92.8	91.3	**99.1***	98.4	87.3	70.9	95.1	90.7	73.8	94.0	94.2	94.3	*
Precision	97.8	97.9	99.6	99.8	99.4	87.3	98.3	97.1	93.5	99.0	97.7	99.1	*
Recall	88.3	85.5	98.7	97.1	77.8	59.6	92.2	85.0	60.9	89.4	90.8	90.0	*
Margin scoring, *intersection*, threshold = 1.20 (*F1*)	88.9	83.9	97.1	93.3	58.8	56.0	91.5	85.8	57.6	86.6	87.6	87.6	*
Precision	98.8	98.9	100	100	98.8	91.3	99.6	99.4	99.8	99.5	97.4	99.5	*
Recall	80.8	72.8	94.4	87.5	41.9	40.4	84.6	75.5	40.5	76.7	79.6	78.2	*
Margin scoring, *intersection*, en-xx (*F1*)	93.0	89.8	98.5	97.5	85.9	*	94.8	93.5	*	*	92.9	93.6	*
Precision	98.2	95.4	99.1	99.2	95.8	*	98.2	98.7	*	*	98.4	98.2	*
Recall	88.3	84.8	97.9	95.8	77.8	*	91.6	88.8	*	*	88.0	89.5	*
Margin scoring, *intersection*, xx-en (*F1*)	**93.7**	**93.9**	97.6	**99.4**	**97.0**	*	**95.5**	**95.2**	*	*	**97.2**	**97.2**	*
Precision	97.5	97.7	99.1	99.9	99.5	*	98.6	97.8	*	*	97.9	98.8	*
Recall	90.2	90.4	96.2	98.9	94.6	*	92.5	92.8	*	*	96.5	95.8	*
Margin scoring, *intersection*, strict intersection (*F1*)	92.0	89.9	97.4	97.6	79.9	*	93.7	91.2	*	*	91.3	92.7	*
Precision	99.2	99.5	99.6	100	100	*	99.7	100	*	*	98.4	99.6	*
Recall	85.7	81.9	95.3	95.3	66.5	*	88.5	83.9	*	*	85.2	86.7	*
Margin scoring, *intersection*, majority vote (*F1*)	93.7	92.5	**99.1***	98.8	94.0	*	95.4	93.6	*	*	95.7	95.9	*
Precision	98.6	97.9	99.6	100	100	*	98.7	99.2	*	*	98.5	99.1	*
Recall	89.3	87.6	98.7	97.6	88.7	*	92.3	88.6	*	*	93.0	92.8	*

Table 4: Tatoeba test set results for a subset of low-resource, English-aligned language pairs, broken down by the mining method used. These language pairs are ones *without* parallel data for the multilingual distillation process described in Reimers and Gurevych (2020) (cf. Table 10 in that paper). Note that LaBSE has training data for most of these languages. Descriptions of the various mining methods are found in Section 4.

EM Corpus: a comparable corpus for a less-resourced language pair Manipuri-English

Rudali Huidrom **Yves Lepage**
IPS, Waseda University
Kitakyushu, Japan
{rudali.huidrom@ruri.,yves.lepage@}waseda.jp

Khogendra Khomdram
The Sangai Express
Manipur, India
khogen.kh@gmail.com

Abstract

In this paper, we introduce a sentence-level comparable text corpus crawled and created for the less-resourced language pair, Manipuri (mni) and English (eng). Our monolingual corpora comprise 1.88 million Manipuri sentences and 1.45 million English sentences, and our parallel corpus comprises 124,975 Manipuri-English sentence pairs. These data were crawled and collected over a year from August 2020 to March 2021 from a local newspaper website called 'The Sangai Express.' The resources reported in this paper are made available to help the low-resourced languages community for MT/NLP tasks[1].

1 Introduction

The web is immense, free, and available to all (Kilgarriff and Grefenstette, 2003). Several studies have proposed the use of the web as a corpus for teaching and research (Rundell, 2000; Robb, 2003; Fletcher, 2001, 2004; Kilgarriff and Grefenstette, 2003). Languages such as English and Chinese are widely published and are well-equipped with resources and tools. Availability of data for low-resource languages on the web is increasing day by day (Schryver, 2002) contributing hugely to bridge the gap between high-resource and low-resource languages. In addition, it is important to mention the language in discussion states #BenderRule (Bender, 2019) to minimize the existing divide of languages in NLP. In this paper, our work is to equip a less-resourced language pair, Manipuri–English with resources.

Our objective is to increase the size of available data for Manipuri–English language pairs. Our goal is to build a sentence-level comparable corpus for Manipuri–English[2] from a newspaper website called *"The Sangai Express"*.[3] We introduce the creation of a comparable corpus named "***Ema-lon Manipuri Corpus***", (translation: our mother tongue Manipuri Corpus) abbreviated as the **EM Corpus**, of the low-resourced language pair, Manipuri–English. We report on the method for creating the comparable corpus. We also tried to extract parallel corpus from our comparable data. Additionally, we provide the table that maps the corresponding glyph points to its Unicode codepoints for Manipuri.

The structure of the paper is as follows. Section 2 describes previous work. Sections 3 and 4 describes the characteristics of the language and the data. Section 5 presents the methodological aspects. Section 6 provides the details of the experiment and its analysis. Section 7 concludes and proposes future directions.

2 Related Work

Several works on the web as a corpus (Rundell, 2000; Robb, 2003; Fletcher, 2001, 2004; Kilgarriff and Grefenstette, 2003) for many languages have been reported from the past decades (Schryver, 2002). The use of web-based Manipuri corpus has been reported by Singh and Bandyopadhyay (2010) for the identification of reduplicated multi-word expression (MWE) and multi-word named entity recognition (NER). PMIndia is yet another crawled data set of 13 Indian languages with English. This data set includes Manipuri–English language pair data. IndicCorp, sourced from news crawls, is a large monolingual corpus of 11 Indian languages from two different language families (Indo-Aryan branch and Dravidian) (Kakwani et al., 2020). Some of the familiar datasets obtained from web crawls are The Leipzig corpus (Goldhahn et al., 2012), CommonCrawl, and The OSCAR project (Ortiz Suárez et al., 2019), none of which contains the Manipuri–English language pair in it.

[1]The corpus is available from http://lepage-lab.ips.waseda.ac.jp/en/projects/meiteilon-manipuri-language-resources/

[2]The codes from ISO 639-2 for these languages are as follows: Manipuri (mni) and English (eng)

[3]https://www.thesangaiexpress.com/

Proceedings of 14th Workshop on Building and Using Comparable Corpora in conjunction with RANLP-2021, pages 60–67, held online, 6 September 2021.
https://doi.org/10.26615/978-954-452-076-2_008

Fung and Cheung (2004) analyses different types of bilingual corpora, ranging from parallel, noisy parallel, comparable, very-non-parallel corpora. Types of comparable corpus includes: (i) non-sentence-aligned, non-translated bilingual documents that are topic-aligned. Example, newspaper articles that are published on the same date in different languages, and (ii) non-aligned sentences that are mostly bilingual translations of the same document. Our work is close to the former.

3 Manipuri (Meiteilon)

Manipuri, locally known as Meiteilon, is an Indian language from the Sino-Tibetan language family. It is highly agglutinative in nature. Manipuri follows the SOV (Subject-Object-Verb) syntax structure. As the predominant language of the Indian state Manipur, Manipuri has about two million native speakers. As a language classified as 'vulnerable language' by UNESCO (Moseley and Nicolas, 2010), it is one of the two Indian languages listed in the 8th Schedule of the Indian Constitution as endangered.

Manipuri has two writing systems: Eastern Nagari Script (also known as the Bengali Script) and Meitei Mayek. We use Manipuri written in Eastern Nagari Script for all of our works. Again, Manipuri is a low-resourced language that has not been explored much in computational linguistics. One of the reasons being the limited amount of available resources. In this paper, we aim to bridge this gap by sharing our resources publicly.

4 Ema-lon Manipuri Corpus (EM Corpus)

The amount of resources for Manipuri–English language pair is limited for performing Machine Translation (MT)/Natural Language Processing (NLP) tasks (Huidrom and Lepage, 2020). For example, there are 41,669 sentences monolingually and 7,419 parallel sentences with English in the open-sourced monolingual and parallel data from the pmindia dataset[4] (Haddow and Kirefu, 2020). Other sources include TDIL-DC[5], where the data is available upon an undertaking agreement. A standard site such as OPUS[6] (Tiedemann, 2012) is limited in the coverage of low-resource Asian and South Asian Languages including, Manipuri. This motivated us to create our comparable corpus.

EM Corpus is built for Manipuri–English language pair. This corpus is created by collecting news articles daily from a newspaper website known as "The Sangai Express," which is available in both languages. An average of 14,000 sentences is crawled for this language pair daily. The reported data is being collected from August 2020 to March 2021, as shown in Figure 1. The domain of the EM Corpus includes general articles, news on state, national and international affairs, sports and entertainment news, and the editorial. The English articles are topic-aligned with the Manipuri articles, however, they are not the exact bilingual translation of each other but rather the summary or the gist of the Manipuri news.

The monolingual datasets contain 1.88 million Manipuri sentences and 1.45 million English sentences and the parallel corpora contain 124,975 sentences. The number of words per sentence in Manipuri and English is reported to be 17 and 23 monolingually and, 21 and 26 in parallel. It is to note that the number of word types in each language reflects the number of sentences and the structure of the language: it is natural that the more the sentence pairs, the higher the number of word types as reported in Table 1. It is reported that the average word length of Manipuri is more than that of English monolingually and in parallel, however, the average word types length is the same for both the languages.

5 Methodology

In this section, we introduce the creation of EM corpus and extraction of parallel corpus from the comparable data.

- **Crawling and Extraction.** The news articles which are available in both languages were crawled and extracted on a daily basis. The news updates in 'The Sangai Express' are available in a section-based format and, each section contains articles in an infinite scroll format. The request for the lists of URLs follows a simple form, and so we source our data with a web scraper for each language which we built. Since the class in the HTML of each article corresponds to each other, document alignment was straightforward. Figure 1 shows the statistics of the data collection obtained per month from August 2020

[4] http://data.statmt.org/pmindia/
[5] https://www.tdil-dc.in/
[6] http://opus.nlpl.eu/index.php

Data set	Language pair	sentences	words	words / sent.	word length	word types	word types length
Monolingual	Manipuri	1,880,035	31,124,061	17	6	95,380	8
	English	1,450,053	33,667,493	23	5	108,812	8
Parallel	Manipuri	124,975	2,589,109	21	6	74,516	8
	English		3,289,671	26	5	64,501	8

Table 1: Detailed statistics on the EM Corpus.

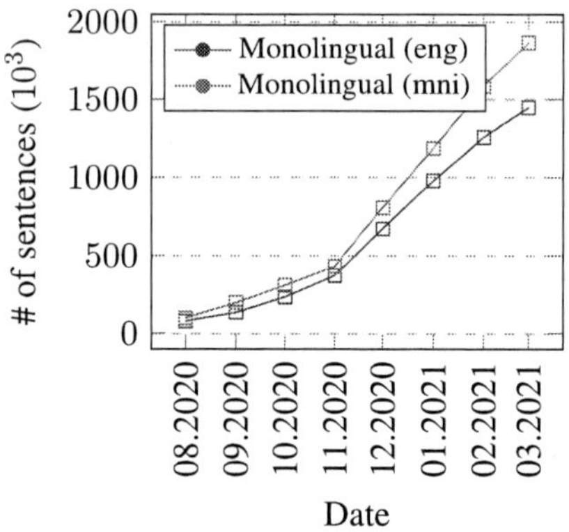

(a) Statistics of the monolingual data collected from August 2020 to March 2021.

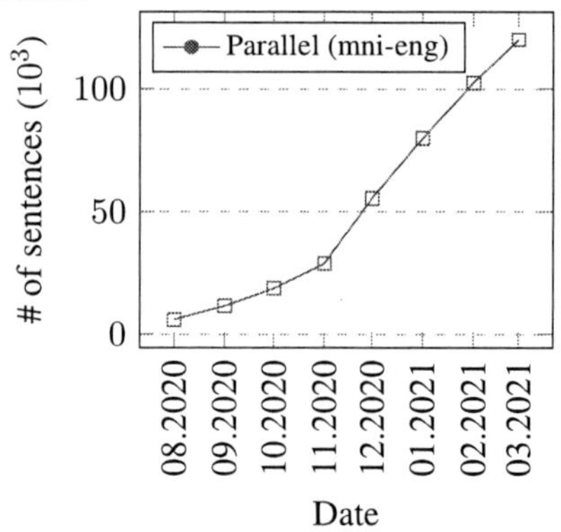

(b) Statistics of the parallel data collected from August 2020 to March 2021.

Figure 1: Statistics of the monolingual and parallel data from the EM Corpus.

to March 2021. To extract the content of the articles from the HTML, we use BeautifulSoup[7] (Richardson, 2007) which is a rich python library for parsing HTML/XML documents, which on inspection performs well in extracting the body of the articles. Additionally, we use cronTab (Reznick, 1993) to automate our news crawl.

[7]https://www.crummy.com/software/BeautifulSoup

- **Text Processing.** The data crawled for Manipuri encoded in nature as the website uses its custom web font file for Manipuri. To obtain the correct text for Manipuri, we map the glyph points to the exact Unicode codepoints. We identified the corresponding matches in this process manually. After obtaining the precise format of the font for Manipuri, we split the articles into sentences for sentence alignment using Moses splitter (Koehn et al., 2007) by taking into account about the sentence delimiter, punctuation, and list items of Manipuri in Eastern Nagari script (Bengali script).

- **Sentence Alignment.** We use Hunalign (Varga et al., 2005), a sentence aligner that aligns bilingual text based on the heuristics of sentence-length information and a bilingual dictionary (if available). It is to be noted that Hunalign does not deal with changes of sentence order like most sentence aligners. Due to the absence of the dictionary for Manipuri, we use the automatic dictionary built based on the alignment. We retain 1-1 alignments obtained from filtering sentences with a threshold that discards score lower than 0.3.

6 Experiment and result

The paper discusses the creation of a comparable corpus from scratch and extracts parallel sentences from the comparable data. As mentioned earlier, the nature of the sentences in the two documents is such that the English news provides a summary of the Manipuri news. Although our documents are topic-aligned, the sentences are not present in a one-to-one correspondence. This explains the difference in the number of sentences monolingually.

Further, we use Hunalign to extract the parallel sentences from EM corpus. We wanted to study the relevance of the parallel sentences extracted

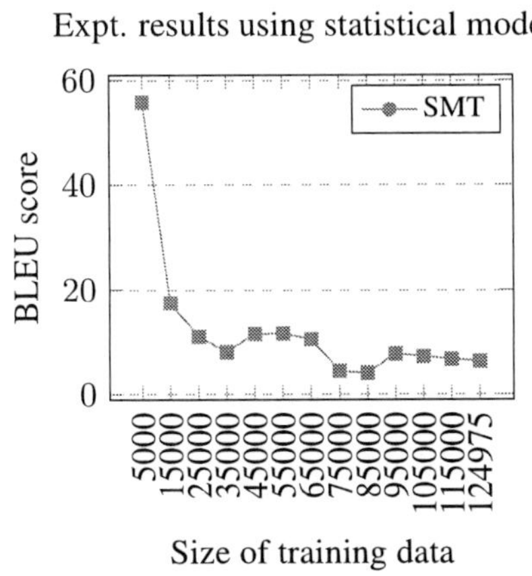

Figure 2: The results are from the SMT experiments (square and brown).

from the comparable data of the aforementioned nature. We designed a simple experiment on statistical machine translation. The models were trained on 5,000 sentences from PMIndia dataset and incremented by 10,000 parallel sentences from our EM corpus in each iteration. Our validation and test data are from the PMIndia (Haddow and Kirefu, 2020) dataset whose domain is the official documents from the Prime Minister Office of India. Figure 2 shows the result of the experiment.

As we progress with the adding of more training data, we observe a decrease in the BLEU score which is expected. It is to be noted that the decrease is not linear in nature. The data that we add other than the baseline are obtained from the news crawls which are not standardised translated data. Although, the sentences are aligned, the parallel sentences are not exact translations of one another, instead comparable. The sudden increase of the BLEU score could be the result of seeing similar sentences crawled from the news articles related to the Prime Minister Office while training.

7 Conclusion

This work provided an insight into corpus creation for Manipuri–English language pair. Firstly, we studied the creation of the comparable corpus, EM corpus for the low-resourced language pair Manipuri–English. Secondly, we discussed the nature of the comparable corpus for Manipuri-English language pair. We report the statistics on these data which is built by collecting from the web for over a year, from August 2020 to March 2021. The appendices provide information on mapping the glyph points to the Unicode codepoints for Manipuri. This is a necessary step due to the nature of the news articles that were crawled. The Sangai Express uses its custom web font file. This table can be referred if you are crawling independently to build your own corpus.

In the future, we would like to inspect the possibility of increasing the size of data by using data-augmentation techniques. Also, we welcome everyone in improving and contributing to these resources.

References

Emily Bender. 2019. The benderrule: On naming the languages we study and why it matters. *The Gradient*.

William H. Fletcher. 2001. Concordancing the web with KWiCFinder. In *In Third North American Symposium on Corpus Linguistics and Language Teaching*, pages 1–16, Boston, MA.

William H. Fletcher. 2004. Making the web more useful as a source for linguistic corpora. *Applied Corpus Linguistics: A multi-dimensional perspective*, 52:191–205.

Pascale Fung and Percy Cheung. 2004. Mining very-non-parallel corpora: Parallel sentence and lexicon extraction via bootstrapping and E. In *Proceedings of the 2004 Conference on Empirical Methods in Natural Language Processing*, pages 57–63, Barcelona, Spain. Association for Computational Linguistics.

Dirk Goldhahn, Thomas Eckart, and Uwe Quasthoff. 2012. Building large monolingual dictionaries at the Leipzig corpora collection: From 100 to 200 languages. In *Proceedings of the Eighth International Conference on Language Resources and Evaluation (LREC'12)*, pages 759–765, Istanbul, Turkey. European Language Resources Association (ELRA).

Barry Haddow and Faheem Kirefu. 2020. Pmindia - a collection of parallel corpora of languages of india. *ArXiv*, abs/2001.09907.

Rudali Huidrom and Yves Lepage. 2020. Zero-shot translation among Indian languages. In *Proceedings of the 3rd Workshop on Technologies for MT of Low Resource Languages*, pages 47–54, Suzhou, China. Association for Computational Linguistics.

Divyanshu Kakwani, Anoop Kunchukuttan, Satish Golla, Gokul N.C., Avik Bhattacharyya, Mitesh M. Khapra, and Pratyush Kumar. 2020. IndicNLPSuite: Monolingual corpora, evaluation benchmarks and pre-trained multilingual language models for Indian languages. In *Findings of the Association for Computational Linguistics: EMNLP 2020*, pages 4948–4961, Online. Association for Computational Linguistics.

Adam Kilgarriff and Gregory Grefenstette. 2003. Introduction to the special issue on the web as corpus. *Computational linguistics*, 29(3):333–347.

Philipp Koehn, Hieu Hoang, Alexandra Birch, Chris Callison-Burch, Marcello Federico, Nicola Bertoldi, Brooke Cowan, Wade Shen, Christine Moran, Richard Zens, Chris Dyer, Ondřej Bojar, Alexandra Constantin, and Evan Herbst. 2007. Moses: Open source toolkit for statistical machine translation. In *Proceedings of the 45th Annual Meeting of the Association for Computational Linguistics Companion Volume Proceedings of the Demo and Poster Sessions*, pages 177–180, Prague, Czech Republic. Association for Computational Linguistics.

Christopher Moseley and Alexandre Nicolas. 2010. *Atlas of the world's languages in danger*, 3 edition. UNESCO, France.

Pedro Javier Ortiz Suárez, Benoît Sagot, and Laurent Romary. 2019. Asynchronous pipelines for processing huge corpora on medium to low resource infrastructures. In *Proceedings of the Workshop on Challenges in the Management of Large Corpora (CMLC-7) 2019. Cardiff, 22nd July 2019*, pages 9 – 16, Mannheim. Leibniz-Institut für Deutsche Sprache.

Larry Reznick. 1993. Using cron and crontab. *Sys Admin*, 2(4):29–32.

Leonard Richardson. 2007. Beautiful soup documentation. *April*.

Thomas N. Robb. 2003. Google as a corpus tool? *ETJ Journal*, 4(1):20–21.

Michael Rundell. 2000. The biggest corpus of all. *Humanising language teaching*, 2(3).

Gilles-Maurice de Schryver. 2002. Web for/as Corpus: A Perspective for the African Languages. *Nordic Journal of African Studies*, 11(2):266–282.

Thoudam Doren Singh and Sivaji Bandyopadhyay. 2010. Web based Manipuri corpus for multiword NER and reduplicated MWEs identification using SVM. In *Proceedings of the 1st Workshop on South and Southeast Asian Natural Language Processing*, pages 35–42, Beijing, China. Coling 2010 Organizing Committee.

Jörg Tiedemann. 2012. Parallel data, tools and interfaces in OPUS. In *Proceedings of the Eighth International Conference on Language Resources and Evaluation (LREC'12)*, pages 2214–2218, Istanbul, Turkey. European Language Resources Association (ELRA).

D. Varga, L. Németh, P. Halácsy, A. Kornai, V. Trón, and V. Nagy. 2005. Parallel corpora for medium density languages. In *In Proceedings of the RANLP 2005*, pages 590–596, Prague, Czech Republic.

Encoded glyph points	’ ’	’!’	’"’	’#’	’$’	’%’	’&’	"’"	’(’	’)’
correct Unicode	\u0020	\u0021	\u0985	\u0988	\u098A	\u0025	\u098F	\u0990	\u0028	\u0029
Encoded glyph points	’*’	’+’	’,’	’-’	’.’	’/’	’0’	’1’	’2’	’3’
correct Unicode	\u0993	\u0994	\u002C	\u002D	\u002E	\u09ac \u09cd \u200d	\u09E6	\u09E7	\u09E8	\u09E9
Encoded glyph points	’4’	’5’	’6’	’7’	’8’	’9’	’:’	’;’	’=’	’>’
correct Unicode	\u09EA	\u09EB	\u09EC	\u09ED	\u09EE	\u09EF	\u003A	\u09CE	\u09A5	\u09A8
Encoded glyph points	’?’	’@’	’A’	’B’	’C’	’D’	’E’	’F’	’G’	’H’
correct Unicode	\u003F	\u0983	\u0995	\u0995 \u09cd \u0995	\u0995 \u09cd \u099f	\u0995 \u09cd \u09a4 \u09cd \u09ac	\u0995 \u09cd \u09ac	\u0995 \u09cd \u09ae	\u0995 \u09cd \u09b8	\u200d \u09cd \u0995
Encoded glyph points	’I’	’J’	’K’	’L’	’M’	’N’	’O’	’P’	’Q’	’R’
correct Unicode	\u0995 \u09cd \u09b0	\u0996	\u0997 \u09cd	\u0997 \u09cd \u0997	\u0997 \u09cd \u09ac	\u0997	\u0997 \u09cd \u200d	\u0997 \u09c1	\u0998	\u0999
Encoded glyph points	’S’	’T’	’U’	’V’	’W’	’X’	’Y’	’Z’	’[’	’\\’
correct Unicode	\u0999 \u09cd \u0995	\u0999 \u09cd \u0996	\u0999 \u09cd \u0997	\u0999 \u09cd \u200d	\u099a	\u09a8 \u09cd \u09b8	\u099a \u09cd \u099b \u09cd \u09ac	\u099a \u09cd \u200d	\u09BF	\u099C
Encoded glyph points	’]’	’^’	’_’	’‘’	’a’	’b’	’c’	’d’	’e’	’f’
correct Unicode	\u09d7 \u0981	\u099c \u09cd \u099c \u09cd \u09ac	\u099c \u09cd \u099d	\u099c \u09cd \u099e	\u099c \u09cd \u09ac	\u099c \u09cd \u09b0	\u099D	\u099E	\u099e \u09cd \u099a	\u099e \u09cd \u099b

Table 2: This table illustrates the correct Unicode format for the encoded glyph points (Part-1).

Encoded glyph points	'g'	'h'	'i'	'j'	'k'	'l'	'm'	'n'	'o'	'p'
correct Unicode	\u099e \u09cd \u099c	\u099e \u09cd \u099d	\u099F	\u099f \u09cd \u099f	\u09A0	\u0989	\u09a1 \u09cd \u09a1	\u09A2	\u09A3	\u09a3 \u09cd \u09a3
Encoded glyph points	'q'	'r'	's'	't'	'u'	'v'	'w'	'x'	'y'	'z'
correct Unicode	\u200d \u09a3 \u09cd \u09a0	\u09a3 \u09cd \u09a1	\u09a3 \u09cd \u200d	\u09A4	\u09a4 \u09cd \u09ae	\u09a4 \u09cd \u09a4	\u09a4 \u09cd \u09a4 \u09cd \u09ac	\u09a4 \u09cd \u09a5	\u09a4 \u09cd \u09b0	\u200d \u09cd \u09a4
Encoded glyph points	'{'	'¦'	'}'	'~'	'\x81'	'\x90'	'\xa0'	'¡'	'¢'	'£'
correct Unicode	\u09bf \u0981	\u098F	\u0982	\u09a4 \u09cd \u09ac	\u09ac \u09cd \u09a2	\u099a \u09cd \u099e	\u00A0	\u200D	\u09b0 \u09cd	\u09ab
Encoded glyph points	'¤'	'¥'	'¦'	'§'	'¨'	'©'	'ª'	'«'	'¬'	'\xad'
correct Unicode	\u09ac	\u200d \u0981	\u09ac \u09cd \u09a6	\u09ac \u09cd \u09a7	\u09ac \u09cd \u099d	\u09b9 \u09cd	\u09ac \u09cd \u099c	\u09ac \u09cd \u200d	\u200d \u09cd \u09ac	\u09a8 \u09cd
Encoded glyph points	'®'	'¯'	'°'	'±'	'²'	'³'	'´'	'µ'	'¶'	'¸'
correct Unicode	\u09AD	\u09F1	\u09ad \u09cd \u09b0	\u200d \u09cd \u09ad	\u200d \u09cd \u09ad \u09cd \u09b0	\u09AE	\u09ae \u09cd	\u200d \u09cd \u09ae	\u200d \u09cd \u09ae	\u200d \u09cd \u09af
Encoded glyph points	'¹'	'º'	'»'	'¼'	'½'	'¾'	'¿'	'À'	'Á'	'Â'
correct Unicode	\u09B0	\u09B2	\u200d \u09b2 \u09cd \u0995	\u200d \u09b2 \u09cd \u0997	\u200d \u200d \u09b2 \u09cd \u0997 \u09c1	\u09b2 \u09cd \u09ac	\u09b2 \u09cd \u09aa	\u09b2 \u09cd \u09b2	\u09b2 \u09cd \u09a1	\u09b2 \u09cd \u200d
Encoded glyph points	'Ã'	'Ä'	'Å'	'Æ'	'Ç'	'È'	'É'	'Ê'	'Ë'	'Ì'
correct Unicode	\u200d \u09cd \u09b2	\u09a8 \u09cd \u09a8	\u09b6	\u09b6 \u09cd \u200d	\u09b6 \u09c1	\u09b7	\u09b7 \u09cd \u200d \u09ac	\u09b7 \u09cd \u099f	\u09b7 \u09cd \u09a0	\u09b7 \u09cd \u09a3

Table 3: This table illustrates the correct Unicode format for the encoded glyph points (Part-2).

Encoded glyph points	'Í'	'Î'	'Ï'	'Ð'	'Ñ'	'Ò'	'Ó'	'Ô'	'Õ'	'Ö'
correct Unicode	\u09b7 \u09cd \u200d	\u09b8	\u09b8 \u09cd \u0996	\u09b8 \u09cd \u099f	\u09b8 \u09cd \u200d	\u09B9	\u09b9 \u09cd \u09b2	\u09b9 \u200d \u09cd \u09ac	\u09b9 \u09cd \u09ae	\u09b9 \u09cd \u09a3
Encoded glyph points	'×'	'Ø'	'Ù'	'Ú'	'Û'	'Ü'	'Ý'	'Þ'	'ß'	'à'
correct Unicode	\u09b9 \u09c1	\u09BC	\u09aa \u09cd \u09aa	\u09DF	\u0995 \u09cd \u09b7	\u0995 \u09cd \u09b7 \u09cd \u09ae	\u0995 \u09cd \u09b7 \u09cd \u09a8	\u09a8 \u09cd \u09ac	\u09aa \u09cd \u09b0	\u09BE
Encoded glyph points	'á'	'â'	'ã'	'ä'	'å'	'æ'	'ç'	'è'	'é'	'ê'
correct Unicode	\u099B	\u09A4	\u09C0	\u09a6 \u09cd \u09a6 \u09cd \u09ac	\u09C1	\u09C1	\u09c1	\u09C2	\u09C2	\u09c2
Encoded glyph points	'ë'	'ì'	'í'	'î'	'ï'	'ð'	'ñ'	'ò'	'ó'	'ô'
correct Unicode	\u09C7	\u09C7	\u09C8	\u09C8	\u09D7	\u099c \u09cd \u099c	\u0993	\u0981	\u09AB	\u09CD
Encoded glyph points	'õ'	'ö'	'÷'	'ø'	'ù'	'ú'	'û'	'ü'	'ý'	'þ'
correct Unicode	\u09C3	\u200d \u09cd \u09b0	\u200d \u09cd \u09b0	\u200d \u09cd \u09b0	\u200d \u09cd \u09b0	\u200C	\u200d	\u200d	\u09c2	\u200d
Encoded glyph points	'ÿ'	'Œ'	'œ'	'Š'	'š'	'Ÿ'	'ƒ'	'ˆ'	'˜'	'–'
correct Unicode	\u200d	\u09a7 \u09cd \u09ae	\u09aa \u09cd \u09a4	\u09a6 \u09cd	\u09aa	\u09aa \u09cd \u200d	\u09a6	\u09a6 \u09cd \u09ae	\u09b8 \u09cd \u09a7	\u09a8 \u09cd \u200d
Encoded glyph points	'—'	'‘'	'’'	'‚'	'“'	'”'	'„'	'†'	'‡'	'•'
correct Unicode	\u200d \u09cd \u09a8	\u2018	\u2019	\u09b9 \u09cd \u200d	\u09a8 \u09cd \u09a1	\u09a8 \u09cd	\u09a6 \u09cd \u09a6	\u09a6 \u09cd \u09a7 \u09cd \u09ac	\u09a6 \u09cd \u09ac	\u200d \u09cd \u09a8
Encoded glyph points	'…'	'‰'	'‹'	'›'	'™'	'\uf000'				
correct Unicode	\u09c0 \u0981	\u09a6 \u09cd \u09b0	\u09a7	\u09aa \u09cd \u09b8	\u09AF	\u200d				

Table 4: This table illustrates the correct Unicode format for the encoded glyph points (Part-3).

On Pronunciations in Wiktionary: Extraction and Experiments on Multilingual Syllabification and Stress Prediction

Winston Wu and **David Yarowsky**
Center for Language and Speech Processing
Johns Hopkins University
{wswu,yarowsky}@jhu.edu

Abstract

We constructed parsers for five non-English editions of Wiktionary, which combined with pronunciations from the English edition, comprises over 5.3 million IPA pronunciations, the largest pronunciation lexicon of its kind. This dataset is a unique comparable corpus of IPA pronunciations annotated from multiple sources. We analyze the dataset, noting the presence of machine-generated pronunciations. We develop a novel visualization method to quantify syllabification. We experiment on the new combined task of multilingual IPA syllabification and stress prediction, finding that training a massively multilingual neural sequence-to-sequence model with copy attention can improve performance on both high- and low-resource languages, and multi-task training on stress prediction helps with syllabification.

1 Introduction

Wiktionary[1] is a free online multilingual dictionary containing a plethora of interesting information. In this paper, we focus on the pronunciation annotations in Wiktionary, which are relatively understudied. For any given word, Wiktionary may include data for IPA (both phonetic and phonemic), hyphenation, dialectical variation, and even audio files of speakers pronouncing the words. These types of data have been shown to be useful for tasks such as grapheme-to-phoneme transduction, e.g. in recent SIGMORPHON shared tasks (Gorman et al., 2020). There are many existing parsing efforts that have extracted pronunciation information from Wiktionary. Recent extractions of data from Wiktionary focus on obtaining high-quality pronunciations from a *single* edition of Wiktionary, usually the English edition (e.g. Wu and Yarowsky, 2020a; Sajous et al., 2020; Lee et al., 2020). However, substantial increases in data can be obtained by parsing other editions of Wiktionary, which have been shown to be helpful for downstream tasks. For example, Schlippe et al. (2010) extract pronunciations from the English, French, German, and Spanish editions, and **?** extract pronunciations from the English, German, Greek, Japanese, Korean, and Russian editions.

In this paper, we build upon Yawipa (Wu and Yarowsky, 2020a,b), a recent Wiktionary parsing framework. Targeting the larger Wiktionaries for increased coverage and those not dealt with in previous work, we construct new pronunciation parsers for the French, Spanish, Malagasy, Italian, and Greek editions of Wiktionary. Combined with pronunciations from the English Wiktionary, this totals to over 5.3 million words, which to our knowledge is the largest pronunciation lexicon to date and also a unique comparable corpora of pronunciations. In Section 2, we show that our extracted pronunciations are a substantial increase in data, covering numerous pronunciations not in the English Wiktionary. This is especially beneficial for low-resource languages. In Section 3, we analyze this data and find that a small portion of these pronunciations may be low-quality and computer-generated. In Section 4, we present a novel visualization technique for analyzing the use of stress in IPA pronunciations. In Section 5, we experiment on the combined task of massively multilingual syllabification and stress detection. Our neural sequence-to-sequence model with copy attention outperforms a sequence labeling baseline, especially in very low-resource scenarios, underscoring the contributions of additional languages to the task. In addition we find that a multi-task approach of predicting both stress and syllabification can improve the performance on syllabification alone.

[1] www.wiktionary.org

Proceedings of 14th Workshop on Building and Using Comparable Corpora in conjunction with RANLP-2021, pages 68–74, held online, 6 September 2021.
https://doi.org/10.26615/978-954-452-076-2_009

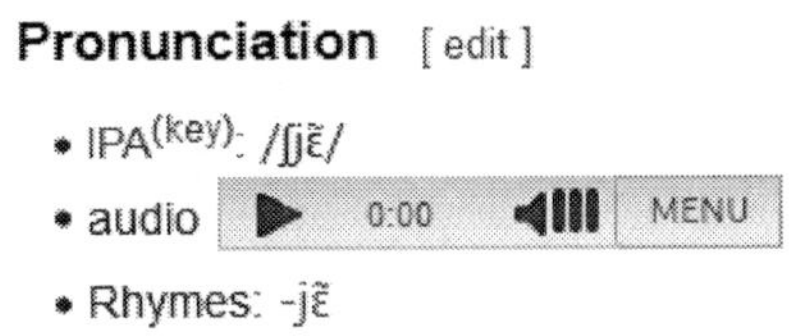

Figure 1: Screenshot of the English Wiktionary's pronunciation information for the French word *chien*.

2 Wiktionary Pronunciation Extraction

As a multilingual resource, Wiktionary exists as a set of numerous *editions*. That is, the English Wiktionary is written in English by and for English speakers, while the French Wiktionary is written in French by and for French speakers. Any edition can contain entries for words in any language. For example, Figure 1 shows a screenshot of the English Wiktionary's pronunciation information for the French word *chien*. We use the terms *<lang> edition* and *<lang> Wiktionary* interchangeably.

Why parse other editions of Wiktionary? Speakers of different languages have different priorities when annotating data. One can assume that an editor of the Spanish Wiktionary is more likely to provide pronunciations for Spanish words before working on English words. Our effort at extracting a new dataset of pronunciations from 6 different editions of Wiktionary resulted in a total of over 5,3 million *unique* IPA pronunciations across 2,177 languages. Note that because the data comes from multiple editions, a word may have multiple annotated pronunciations, making our dataset an interesting comparable corpora. Figure 2 shows the 16 languages with the most data in this dataset, along with the contribution of each edition of Wiktionary from which we parsed and extracted IPA pronunciations.

We draw several insights from Figure 2. First, the inclusion of pronunciations from non-English Wiktionaries represents substantial gains. Though the English edition is the largest Wiktionary by number of entries,[2] the French edition contains a huge number of pronunciations for French words, dwarfing other editions that we parsed. The French Wiktionary also supplies the entirety of the pronunciations for Northern Sami words (`se`, spoken in Norway, Sweden, and Finland), most of the available pronunciations for Esperanto (`eo`) and Italian

[2]https://meta.wikimedia.org/wiki/Wiktionary

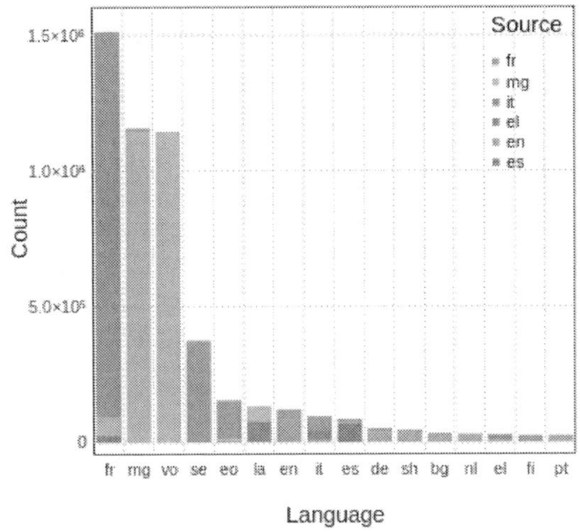

Figure 2: The top 16 languages in terms of number of pronunciations, with contributions from multiple editions of Wiktionary.

(`it`) words, and also words in 1,198 other low-resource languages not shown in the long tail of Figure 2. In contrast, the English edition (the second largest supplier) is the sole supplier of pronunciations in 416 languages.

Parsing Implementation The Yawipa framework (Wu and Yarowsky, 2020a) extracts data from the XML dump of Wiktionary.[3] Every entry is encoded in MediaWiki markup, which is similar to Markdown but includes special *templates* (enclosed in double braces) which programmatically generates HTML that we see when we visit the Wiktionary website. For example, in the English wiktionary, the entry for the French word *chien* contains the following markup (rendered in Figure 1):

```
===Pronunciation===
{{fr-IPA}}
{{audio|fr|Fr-chien.ogg|audio}}
{{rhymes|fr|jɛ̃}}
```

These three templates generate the three bullet points in Figure 1. Note that the `{{fr-IPA}}` template generates the IPA pronunciation, so the IPA itself does not exist in the English Wiktionary dump. Thus, we can only extract the IPA from the French edition, below, highlighting the need to parse multiple Wiktionary editions for multiple sources of pronunciations.

[3]https://dumps.wikimedia.org/enwiktionary/latest/XXwiktionary-latest-pages-articles.xml.bz2, where XX is replaced with a two-letter ISO 639-1 code.

```
=== {{S|nom|fr}} ===
{{fr-rég|ʃjɛ̃}}
```

Above is the French Wiktionary's pronunciation for the word *chien*. A template (`fr-rég`) is also used, but the IPA is extractable from the markup. Each edition of Wiktionary has its own conventions on formatting and templates, thus requiring a separate parser specifically for that edition. For implementation details, please see the repository `https://github.com/wswu/yawipa`.

3 Analysis of the Dataset

For high-resource languages, the home language edition (e.g. English edition for the English language) usually supplies the most pronunciations, but this is not always the case (e.g. the French Wiktionary provides more Italian pronunciations than the Italian edition). In terms of amount of data, two languages are outliers: Malagasy (`mg`, an Austronesian language spoken in Madagascar) and Volapük (`vo`, a constructed language). As relatively less spoken languages, these languages have a disproportionately large amount of data. Why is this so?

The data for these two languages come from the Malagasy edition, which we parsed because of its high ranking in the List of Wiktionaries.[4] Both Malagasy and Volapük are inflected languages[5] whose IPA pronunciations seem to be entirely computer-generated using a regular transduction process from orthography to IPA, which was exploited to create a large set of pronunciations for these two languages.

We also find that some Latin pronunciations may be machine-generated. For example, the Malagasy edition supplies /kontabulawit/ as the pronunciation for the Latin *contabulavit* and [d̪ẽːonstrat] for *demonstrat*. These pronunciations lack stress and syllable markings, and in the case of *demonstrat*, do not agree with established pronunciations of Latin. thus leading us to believe that these were machine-generated pronunciations. In contrast, the English edition contains both well-formed classical and ecclesiastical Latin pronunciations with stress and syllable markers, but only for the dictionary forms *contabulō* /konˈta.bu.loː/ and *dēmonstrō* /deːˈmon.stroː/.

[4] `https://en.wikipedia.org/wiki/List_of_Wiktionaries`

[5] Inflected words have their own Wiktionary entry, which can exponentially increase the number of pronunciations.

We must emphasize that we are not condemning the use of machine-generated pronunciations. For many languages, e.g. Spanish and Latin, the spelling of a word reflects its pronunciation, so generated pronunciations are likely to be accurate. Indeed, the existence of pronunciation templates such as `{{fr-IPA}}`, mentioned above, are well-researched additions to Wiktionary that alleviate the need for humans to manually input IPA pronunciations, thus reducing the potential for human error. We fully support the use of these templates (though they make our parsing job harder), and we would love to see them standardized across all Wiktionary editions, so that editions such as the Malagasy edition can benefit from contributions to the English edition (or any other edition, for that matter).

We do caution researchers that the data contained in crowd-sourced resources such as Wiktionary may not be thoroughly vetted for accuracy, as we have discovered. Fortunately, the openness of these crowdsourced data allows for community members to quickly intervene when problematic data is found. One especially poignant example in recent news is the Scots Wikipedia, a large portion of which was recently revealed to be written by an American teenager who is not a Scots speaker.[6] Essentially, this teenager translated English articles into "Scots" by systematically rewriting English words to sound as if they were spoken with a Scottish accent, in the same vein as some of the Latin "IPA" pronunciations in the Malagasy Wiktionary.

4 Visualizing Syllabification

IPA has the ability to mark syllable boundaries (.) as well as primary (ˈ) and secondary (ˌ) stress. Words in some languages, e.g. Malay, do not have stress, and sometimes stress can be double marked (ˈˈ) for extra stress. We first quantify IPA stress and syllabification in our extracted dataset then present multilingual experiments on predicting syllabification and stress.

We develop a visualization technique to understand the distribution of words in each language that contain syllable boundaries (Figure 3). These bubble charts plot the number of characters in a word (x-axis), the percentage of words containing syllable markers (y-axis), and the number of words

[6] `https://www.reddit.com/r/Scotland/comments/ig9jia/ive_discovered_that_almost_every_single_article`

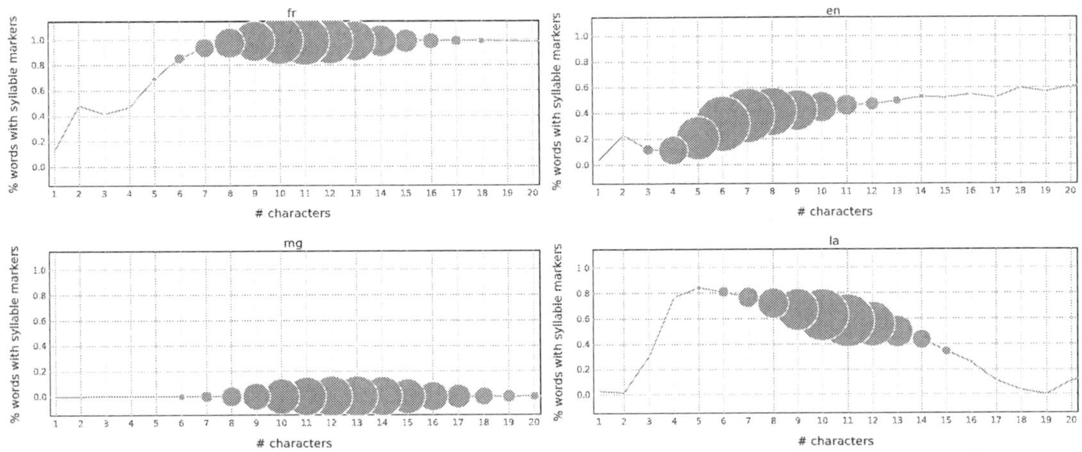

Figure 3: Percentage of French, English, Malagasy, and Latin words containing syllable markers, by length of word. The size of the points indicates the number of words and cannot be compared among graphs.

in these categories (size of the dot). These charts can help researchers to quickly quantify the presence of syllable markers, one component of high-quality IPA pronunciations. We consider a word to be syllabified if it contains any of the following symbols: . ˈ ˌ

Ideally, one should see that the longer the word, the higher the percentage of words that have syllables marked. French is a perfect example of this: once words reach 9–10 characters in length, they all contain syllable markers. By examining these plots, we can easily identify examples of problematic IPA syllabification in Malagasy (`mg`) and Latin (`la`) words. For Malagasy words, syllable boundaries simply do not exist. For Latin words, we see an unusual negative-slope curve, where words around 4–6 characters in length are more likely to have syllables marked, but longer words are less likely to have syllable boundaries marked. This analysis actually is consistent with our earlier finding in Section 2: because Latin is a highly inflected language, the dictionary forms contain high-quality IPA, but the overwhelming number of pronunciations are actually machine-generated for inflected forms, which may not have the syllables marked. English is a middle ground in terms of quality. While we see the expected upward slope as the length of the word increases, the percentage of words with syllable markers never approaches 100%. A manual review of several English pronunciations indicates that annotators simply did not include syllable boundaries for many English words. Further analyses could shed light on the reasons for the negligence of the annotators, or other phenomena that might explain the lack of syllable markers.

5 Experiments

In this section, we present experiments on multilingual syllable and stress prediction. In the linguistics literature, many studies have shown that awareness of syllable boundaries can improve word recognition performance in children (e.g. McBride-Chang et al., 2004; Plaza and Cohen, 2007; Güldeoğlu, 2017). Speech syllabification is also a common step in a speech recognition pipeline. Syllabification of text is not a new task, and has been explored via a variety of methods, including rule-based and grammar-based approaches (e.g. Weerasinghe et al., 2005; Müller, 2006) and data-driven approaches (e.g. Bartlett et al., 2008; Nicolai et al., 2016; Gyanendro Singh et al., 2016). However, previous work has focused primarily on a handful of languages, and some focus on orthographic syllabification rather than phonemic segmentation. Some use CELEX (Baayen et al., 1996), a popular dataset containing syllabified text, but it only contains syllabified words in English, German, and Dutch. In contrast, our extracted pronunciation lexicon is a unique multilingual resource that allows for developing and evaluating models and approaches on the new combined task of massively multilingual IPA syllabification *and* stress prediction across hundreds of languages. In this task, given unmarked IPA, a model must insert syllable markers or stress markers at the appropriate locations.

Data For our task, we filter our pronunciation dataset to keep only IPA containing syllable boundaries or stress markers,[7] so that we have ground truth for our model. This resulted in 93,206 IPA pronunciations across 174 languages, which we split into a 80-10-10 train-dev-test stratified split (same proportion of languages in each set).

Models We first build a baseline: a multilingual character BiLSTM sequence tagger with 256 hidden size (B) that predicts both stress and syllabification (Str & Syl) or syllabification alone (Syl). The data is preprocessed such that each IPA character is labelled with 0 for no stress or syllable, 1 for primary stress (ˈ), 2 for secondary stress (ˌ), and 3 for syllable boundary (.). We include a language token so the model will incorporate knowledge of the language. For example:

IPA: /ˌɪn.fluˈɛn.zə/
Input: `eng ɪ n f l u ɛ n z ə`
Output: `0 2 0 3 0 0 1 0 3 0`

For comparison, we experiment with two modern seq2seq models: the default encoder-decoder model (S) in OpenNMT-py (Klein et al., 2017), and the same model with copy attention (SC) (See et al., 2017). In this scenario, we formulate syllabification and stress prediction as a sequence generation task, where the input is an unstressed, unsyllabified IPA, and the output is the original IPA sequence containing both stress and syllable markers.

We then treat syllabification and stress prediction in a pipelined approach (Syl → Str), where the first model (B or SC) will predict syllable boundaries, and then a second model will predict the stress. Stress classification is a 3-class classification problem: given a syllable, predict primary stress, secondary stress, or no stress. The structure of this stress classifier is also a BiLSTM, where the hidden state of the syllable in question is passed to a dense feed-forward layer, then a softmax.

5.1 Results

A summary of experimental results is in Table 1. The baseline BiLSTM model performs consistently worse than the seq2seq models. This is somewhat surprising, since the seq2seq task is a more challenging task: the model must generate the IPA characters along with stress and syllable markers. However, the seq2seq model is able to generate the

[7]A stress marker can server as a syllable boundary, e.g. for the English word *consume* /kənˈsum/.

Model	Acc	CED	5Acc	5CED
B Syl	68	.48	—	—
SC Syl	79	.42	96	.11
B Syl → Str	53	.88	—	—
SC Syl → Str	31	1.13	—	—
B Str & Syl	52	.89	—	—
-Str	68	.49	—	—
S Str & Syl	69	.72	89	.25
-Str	77	.47	93	.16
SC Str & Syl	74	.54	92	.17
-Str	81	.35	95	.11

Table 1: Results on the syllabification and stress prediction tasks. See Section 5 for abbreviations. Acc is 1-best accuracy, 5Best is 5-best accuracy (is the gold in the top 5 hypotheses?), CED is mean character edit distance.

correct sequence of IPA characters, minus stress and syllable markers, in 95% (for regular attention) and 99% (for copy attention) of test examples, alleviating our concerns and proving the effectiveness of copy attention for this task.

The pipeline approach performs substantially worse than the multi-task approach. In the pipeline, the syllabification model first predicts the syllable boundaries, then the stress classifier produces a classification for each syllable. We find that with the pipeline approach, it is impossible to improve upon the first step in the pipeline. Thus, if the syllabification step does not correctly identify syllable boundaries, the final pronunciation will never be correct, even if the stress is correctly predicted for each syllable.

Finally, multi-task training on both syllabification and stress marking improves performance over syllabification alone. We believe this is because stress and syllable prediction are two somewhat overlapping tasks. If a model can label stress, then it should have some notion of where syllables are. The (-Str) rows in Table 1 show performance on syllabification by evaluating the output of the multitask model preprocessed to replace all stress marks with syllable boundaries.

The large majority of languages in our dataset can be considered low-resource, a specific interest of our experiments. 154 of the 174 languages have much fewer than 466 training examples (0.5% of the entire dataset), yet the average accuracy on these languages is an impressive 67% for syllabification (B Str & Syl - Str) and 51% for both syllabification and stress prediction (B Str & Syl). This highlights the contribution of other languages in a single massively multilingual model trained to do both tasks. Other researchers have found that good performance on syllabification requires much more data than this (Nicolai et al., 2016). We highlight the fact that many of the languages have less than 10 test examples and can be considered truly low-resource; the contribution of many other languages allows our multilingual models to predict the correct pronunciation with minimal training data in a specific language. Though we find that multilingual training helps for low-resource languages, it can also help with high-resource languages: in the SC Str & Syl scenario, a model trained only on French obtained 92.1% on the French test words, compared to the multilingual model at 98.1% accuracy. Full tables of results, along with code to reproduce our experiments, is available at `https://github.com/wswu/syllabification`.

6 Conclusion

We extracted the largest dataset of IPA pronunciations to date, by combining IPA from the French, Spanish, Malagasy, Italian, and Greek editions of Wiktionary along with existing pronunciations from the English edition, totaling to 5.3 million pronunciations. We developed a visualization method for examining syllabification in large datasets, which can give indications about the quality of IPA pronunciations. We experiment on the new combined task of massively multilingual prediction of syllabification and stress using a variety of models and approaches, showing success with a multitask multilingual sequence-to-sequence model. We hope our dataset and analysis methods will be useful for researchers in a variety of disciplines.

We envision our newly extracted pronunciation dataset to be especially useful for researchers interested in lexicography and spoken language technologies. In terms of lexicography, this dataset is a unique comparable corpus containing annotations from several editions of Wiktionary, each representing a distinct population of speakers. In several cases, the same pronunciation is supplied by multiple editions, and some editions use phonetic rather than phonemic IPA. Future work can address questions such as: When and why might different editions disagree on a pronunciation? Why do some words have pronunciations and others don't? In addition, we would like to investigate the use of our pronunciation dataset in language learning of core vocabulary of low-resource languages (Wu et al., 2020) and modeling etymology relationships between words (Wu et al., 2021).

References

R. H. Baayen, R. Piepenbrock, and L. Gulikers. 1996. The celex lexical database (cd-rom).

Susan Bartlett, Grzegorz Kondrak, and Colin Cherry. 2008. Automatic syllabification with structured SVMs for letter-to-phoneme conversion. In *Proceedings of ACL-08: HLT*, pages 568–576, Columbus, Ohio. Association for Computational Linguistics.

Kyle Gorman, Lucas F.E. Ashby, Aaron Goyzueta, Arya McCarthy, Shijie Wu, and Daniel You. 2020. The SIGMORPHON 2020 shared task on multilingual grapheme-to-phoneme conversion. In *Proceedings of the 17th SIGMORPHON Workshop on Computational Research in Phonetics, Phonology, and Morphology*, pages 40–50, Online. Association for Computational Linguistics.

Birkan Güldenoğlu. 2017. The effects of syllable-awareness skills on the word-reading performances of students reading in a transparent orthography. *International Electronic Journal of Elementary Education*, 8(3):425–442.

Loitongbam Gyanendro Singh, Lenin Laitonjam, and Sanasam Ranbir Singh. 2016. Automatic syllabification for Manipuri language. In *Proceedings of COLING 2016, the 26th International Conference on Computational Linguistics: Technical Papers*, pages 349–357, Osaka, Japan. The COLING 2016 Organizing Committee.

G. Klein, Yoon Kim, Y. Deng, Jean Senellart, and Alexander M. Rush. 2017. Opennmt: Open-source toolkit for neural machine translation. *ArXiv*, abs/1701.02810.

Jackson L. Lee, Lucas F.E. Ashby, M. Elizabeth Garza, Yeonju Lee-Sikka, Sean Miller, Alan Wong, Arya D. McCarthy, and Kyle Gorman. 2020. Massively multilingual pronunciation modeling with WikiPron. In *Proceedings of the 12th Language Resources and Evaluation Conference*, pages 4223–4228, Marseille, France. European Language Resources Association.

Catherine McBride-Chang, Ellen Bialystok, Karen KY Chong, and Yanping Li. 2004. Levels of phonological awareness in three cultures. *Journal of Experimental Child Psychology*, 89(2):93–111.

Karin Müller. 2006. Improving syllabification models with phonotactic knowledge. In *Proceedings of the Eighth Meeting of the ACL Special Interest Group on*

Computational Phonology and Morphology at HLT-NAACL 2006, pages 11–20, New York City, USA. Association for Computational Linguistics.

Garrett Nicolai, Lei Yao, and Grzegorz Kondrak. 2016. Morphological segmentation can improve syllabification. In *Proceedings of the 14th SIGMORPHON Workshop on Computational Research in Phonetics, Phonology, and Morphology*, pages 99–103, Berlin, Germany. Association for Computational Linguistics.

Monique Plaza and Henri Cohen. 2007. The contribution of phonological awareness and visual attention in early reading and spelling. *Dyslexia*, 13(1):67–76.

Franck Sajous, Basilio Calderone, and Nabil Hathout. 2020. ENGLAWI: From human- to machine-readable Wiktionary. In *Proceedings of the 12th Language Resources and Evaluation Conference*, pages 3016–3026, Marseille, France. European Language Resources Association.

Tim Schlippe, Sebastian Ochs, and Tanja Schultz. 2010. Wiktionary as a source for automatic pronunciation extraction. In *INTERSPEECH*.

Abigail See, Peter J. Liu, and Christopher D. Manning. 2017. Get to the point: Summarization with pointer-generator networks. In *Proceedings of the 55th Annual Meeting of the Association for Computational Linguistics (Volume 1: Long Papers)*, pages 1073–1083, Vancouver, Canada. Association for Computational Linguistics.

Ruvan Weerasinghe, Asanka Wasala, and Kumudu Gamage. 2005. A rule based syllabification algorithm for Sinhala. In *Second International Joint Conference on Natural Language Processing: Full Papers*.

Winston Wu, Kevin Duh, and David Yarowsky. 2021. Sequence models for computational etymology of borrowings. In *Findings of the Association for Computational Linguistics: ACL-IJCNLP 2021*, pages 4032–4037, Online. Association for Computational Linguistics.

Winston Wu, Garrett Nicolai, and David Yarowsky. 2020. Multilingual dictionary based construction of core vocabulary. In *Proceedings of the 12th Language Resources and Evaluation Conference*, pages 4211–4217, Marseille, France. European Language Resources Association.

Winston Wu and David Yarowsky. 2020a. Computational etymology and word emergence. In *Proceedings of the 12th Language Resources and Evaluation Conference*, pages 3252–3259, Marseille, France. European Language Resources Association.

Winston Wu and David Yarowsky. 2020b. Wiktionary normalization of translations and morphological information. In *Proceedings of the 28th International Conference on Computational Linguistics*, pages 4683–4692, Barcelona, Spain (Online). International Committee on Computational Linguistics.

A Dutch Dataset for Cross-lingual Multi-label Toxicity Detection

Ben Burtenshaw and **Mike Kestemont**
Antwerp Centre for Digital Humanities and Literary Criticism
University of Antwerp
Prinsstraat 13, 2000
Antwerp (Belgium)
firstname.lastname@uantwerpen.be

Abstract

Multi-label toxicity detection is highly prominent, with many research groups, companies, and individuals engaging with it through shared tasks and dedicated venues. This paper describes a cross-lingual approach to annotating multi-label text classification on a newly developed Dutch language dataset, using a model trained on English data. We present an ensemble model of one Transformer model and an LSTM using Multilingual embeddings. The combination of multilingual embeddings and the Transformer model improves performance in a cross-lingual setting.

1 Introduction

Toxic comment detection is becoming an integral part of online discussion, and most major social media platforms use it. However, that success is not shared equally across languages. Low resource languages still lack the accurate pre-trained models that are readily available in more resourced languages, such as English. This is mostly due to a lack of annotated corpora. Inconsistent task definitions of task compound the problem. Where quality data does exist, it often uses alternative task definitions. This paper aims to overcome that challenge by annotating a new dataset and evaluating it within a cross-lingual experiment. We perform multi-label text classification, using an ensemble approach of Transformer and LSTM models with multilingual embeddings (Vaswani et al., 2017; Devlin et al., 2019; Van Hee et al., 2015a). The system is trained on English data by Wulczyn et al. and evaluated on newly annotated Dutch text from the Amica corpus (Wulczyn et al., 2017a; Van Hee et al., 2015a).

We selected multi-label toxicity over other label definitions based on its adaptability and feedback from annotators. Toxicity draws its origins from chemistry, referring to how a substance can damage an organism. From experience in annotator training and feedback, this is a straightforward term to communicate to annotators who relate quickly to the concept of harmful language that degrades a conversation or debate, much like a poison.

2 Related Research

The Conversation AI group defined multi-label toxicity, and Wulczyn et al.(Wulczyn et al., 2017c). The term goes beyond its counterparts by adding fine-grained sub-labels. The original motivation of Wulczyn et al. was for multi-label toxicity to serve as a compatible annotation model for tasks beyond the original Wikipedia dataset. Unlike other similar initiatives, their work focused on the risk that communities break down or turn silent, "leading many communities to limit or completely shut down user comments" (Wulczyn et al., 2017a,c). For a detailed overview of multi-label toxicity, look to van Aken et al., or Gunasekera et al. (Georgakopoulos et al., 2018; Wulczyn et al., 2017b).

A current challenge within the sub-field of toxicity detection is the definition and operationalisation as a concrete task. Though there is research within the area, many projects take up alternative interpretations and definitions. This has led to grey areas between terms like offensive language and profanity, cyberbullying, and online harassment. In practice, many projects are classifying the same data and phenomena under alternative definitions. This problem is explored in greater detail by Emmery and colleagues (Emmery et al., 2019).

Cross-lingual classification uses training material in one language and test material in another. In this paper, we use English language training data to improve performance on Dutch language test data. This resourceful combination relies on recent advancements in multilingual models and benefits underrepresented languages greatly. Data

Proceedings of 14th Workshop on Building and Using Comparable Corpora in conjunction with RANLP-2021, pages 75–79, held online, 6 September 2021.
https://doi.org/10.26615/978-954-452-076-2_010

Negative	94.04	Blackmail	0.11
insult	1.96	Racism	0.1
Harmless_sexual	0.97	Att_relatives	0.09
Curse_Exclusion	0.65	Powerless	0.06
Assertive_selfdef	0.54	Other	0.04
Other_language	0.4	Sarcasm	0.04
Sexual_harassment	0.33	Good	0.01
General_defense	0.33	pro_harasser	0.01
Defamation	0.18	Sexism	0.13

Table 1: Cyberbullying Labels within Amica Dataset and Frequency

sets like that of Conversation AI are less available for Dutch, making classification harder. There are a series of recent projects utilising multilingual pre-trained models for cross-lingual classification of toxic comments (Pamungkas and Patti, 2019; Pant and Dadu, 2020; Stappen et al., 2020).

Amica was a collaborative project between Dutch-speaking NLP research groups into cyberbullying. Van Hee et al. facilitated the detailed annotation of many data sets for a range of bullying labels, using real and simulated conversations between children. Table 1 gives the label distribution.

3 Data

We use a newly annotated version of the AMiCA dataset, initially developed by Van Hee et al., for cyberbullying tasks. In addition, we performed further annotation for multi-label toxicity, following the label guidelines of Wulczyn et al..

3.1 AMiCA Instant Messages

Van Hee et al. developed the AMiCA dataset through anonymous donation and simulation outlined by Emmery et al.. Table 2 reveals the macro details of the data used with original cyberbullying token labels.

Bullying Tokens	2,343
Negative Tokens	2,546
All Tokens	62,340
Mean Tokens per msg	12

Table 2: AMiCA data lexical statistics

3.2 Multi-label Toxicity Annotation

To annotate the AMiCA dataset for Multi-label toxicity labels, we used the annotation instructions outlined in (Wulczyn et al., 2017c). We translated the instructions into Dutch, the native language of the annotators, and gave detailed guidance with an introductory tutorial and handout. Table 3 describes the sub-labels: Toxicity, Severe Toxicity, Identity Attack, Insult, Profanity, and Threat.

TOXICITY Rude, disrespectful, or unreasonable comment that is likely to make people leave a discussion.
SEVERE_TOXICITY A very hateful, aggressive, disrespectful comment or otherwise very likely to make a user leave a discussion.
IDENTITY_ATTACK Negative or hateful comments targeting someone because of their identity.
INSULT Insulting, inflammatory, or negative comment towards a person or a group of people.
PROFANITY Swear words, curse words, or other obscene or profane languages.
THREAT Describes an intention to inflict pain, injury, or violence against an individual or group.

Table 3: Description and Example of labels from the Wikipedia Talk Labels: Toxicity Dataset

We stored the annotated data in a SQL table using the row index of the original AMiCA annotations for cyberbullying. Table 4 shows the distribution of labels across the English data by Wulczyn et al. and the newly annotated data.

Interannotator Agreement We calculated inter-annotator agreement using the largest set of overlapping instances by the same two annotators achieving a **Krippendorf score of 0.4483**, revealing that there was substantial agreement between annotators. We can compare this to that of Wulczyn et al., which scored 0.45 (Wulczyn et al., 2017a). We can delve further into inter-annotator relations through multi-label use. Figure 1 reveals the Cohen Kappa between labels. We see that all six true label pairs (i.e. TOXIC & TOXIC) achieve a fair to substantial correlation and that all false label pairs (i.e. INSULT & THREAT) do not correlate.

	New		Wulczyn 2017	
	n	%	n	%
toxic	3157	31%	15294	44%
severe	833	8%	1596	5%
threat	851	8%	8449	24%
profanity	1165	11%	478	1%
insult	1276	13%	7877	22%
identity	1339	13%	1405	04%
Total	10189		35099	

Table 4: Annotated Labels in Dutch (New) and English (Wulczyn 2017) data. n shows the number of comments for each label and % shows the percentage of the total comments for that label.

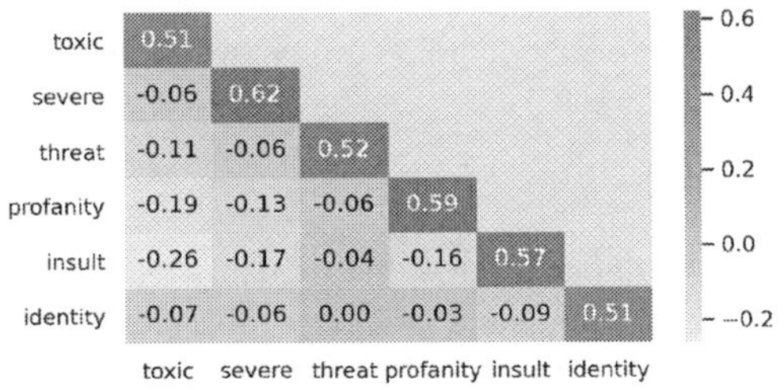

Figure 1: Correlation Matrix of Toxic labels on Annotated Amica Dataset

Compare Toxicity and Cyberbullying As a precursor to the main experiments, and to align the new annotation with Van Hee et al., we tested how cyberbullying acts as a naive predictor of toxicity using the combined labels for each class and F1 Score (Van Hee et al., 2015b; Emmery et al., 2019). We calculated an F1 score of 0.51, revealing that multi-label toxicity does not align with cyberbullying.

4 Method

We performed cross-lingual classification using an Ensemble approach of two component models, a fine-tuned multilingual BERT-base and an LSTM model using Multilingual Unsupervised and Supervised Embeddings (MUSE) (Conneau et al., 2017; Lample et al., 2017). We also used two baseline models for comparison, an LSTM without multilingual embeddings and a Support Vector Machine.

4.1 Fine-tuned BERT-base

We fine-tuned a Multilingual BERT-base model and 3 linear layers. A Bidirectional Encoder Representation from Transformers or BERT model is a pre-trained model that uses bidirectional training to learn contextual attention at a word and sub-word level (Devlin et al., 2019). We used sub-word token representation that aligns with the base vocabulary representation (Zhang et al., 2020). We fine-tuned the BERT model for 4 epochs over a 10-fold cross-validated dataset. The mean validation and training loss for all folds of the data was 0.05.

4.2 LSTM and MUSE Embeddings

We trained a Long Short-term Memory (LSTM) network with Multilingual Universal Sentence Embeddings (MUSE) (Hochreiter and Schmidhuber, 1997; Conneau et al., 2017; Lample et al., 2017). We train the LSTM model for 12 epochs over a 10-fold cross-validated dataset. The mean validation and training loss for all splits of the data was 0.03.

4.3 Ensemble

We used a Random Forest ensemble of the LSTM and BERT models on a cross-validated training set with grid-searched parameters (Breiman, 2001; Nowak et al., 2017). A key risk in ensemble training is overfitting (Pourtaheri and Zahiri, 2016), to mitigate this all models have used a stratified k-fold structure (Yadav and Shukla, 2016).

4.4 Training and Fine-tuning

We used a stratified k-fold configuration of the English and Dutch data to train and fine-tune models. First, we trained and fine-tuned models on a 'train' portion and collected the predicted labels on 'test' portions of the folds, split for English and Dutch data. This allowed us to reveal language performance separately. Next, we trained the ensemble model on component model predictions. Finally, we used an exhaustive grid search to select hyperparameters (Bergstra and Bengio, 2012) and a Receiver Under the Curve analysis (ROC) to select decision thresholds from the component models (Fawcett, 2006).

5 Results

Table 5 reveals results for *baselines*, component models, and ensemble model. We express results as Area Under the Curve, mean Precision, mean Recall, mean F1 for all labels. Baseline models are a Support Vector Machine of Continuous Bag-of-Words representations and an LSTM without Multilingual Universal Sentence Embeddings. Both component models achieved relevant F1 scores for the multi-label classification of toxicity, and the ensemble approach achieved the highest score. We also find that component models were able to overcome the low precision score seen in baseline methods.

	AUC	Pre	Rec	F1
Ensemble	0.9401	0.7023	0.8789	0.7323
BERT	0.9113	0.6745	0.8412	0.7017
MUSE	0.8552	0.6301	0.7838	0.6512
LSTM w/o MUSE	0.7519	0.5692	0.7021	0.5845
SVM & CBOW	0.5702	0.4239	0.5217	0.4419

Table 5: Results Table of *baselines*, component, and ensemble models. Results are expressed as AUC, mean Precision, mean Recall, mean F1 for all labels.

6 Analysis

We performed error analysis to interpret model performance in relation to labels and the language of comments.

Sub-label Performance Figure 2 reveals the Precision, Recall, and F1 Score of the Ensemble model on all labels. Furthermore, we can see that the model performs better at negative label prediction, a common trait in transformer model classification.

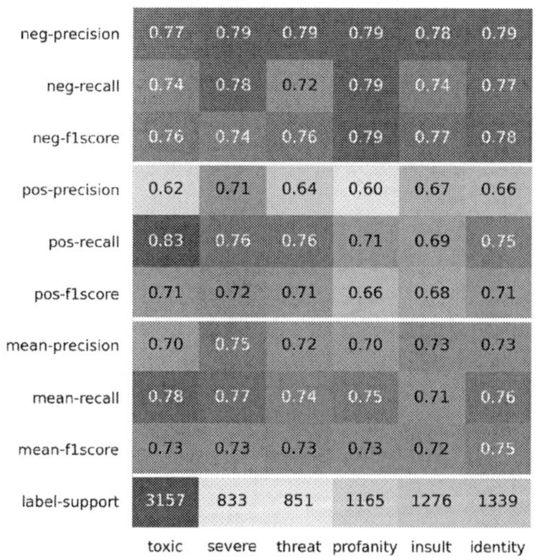

Figure 2: Classification Report from Ensemble Approach on all toxicity labels

Cross-lingual Performance We explored the models' cross-lingual performance by comparing their scores on the English and Dutch data, shown in Table 6. Logically, the LSTM with MUSE embeddings performs poorly on English data, without relevant embedding weights. On the other hand, the BERT model performs well in both languages, and the Ensemble model relies on that when classifying English Data.

	All	EN	NL
Ensemble	0.6401	0.7587	0.7323
BERT	0.7112	0.7213	0.7017
MUSE	0.4812	0.4512	0.6512

Table 6: Cross-lingual Performance: F1 Scores of underlinecomponent and ensemble models. **EN** are scores on the Wulczyn data, **NL** are score on the new Dutch data.

7 Summary

We have demonstrated that by using multilingual pre-trained language models within an ensemble approach, we can classify multi-label toxicity in an alternate language. Furthermore, we have demonstrated that the BERT model's underlying training affects target language performance by analysing the performance of baseline, component and ensemble models in cross-lingual features. Furthermore, Table 5 reveals that component models were able to overcome an excess of false positives that hindered baseline methods.

References

James Bergstra and Yoshua Bengio. 2012. Random Search for Hyper-Parameter Optimization. *Journal of Machine Learning Research* 13 (2012), 25.

Leo Breiman. 2001. Random Forests. *Machine Learning* 45, 1 (Oct. 2001), 5–32. https://doi.org/10.1023/A:1010933404324

Alexis Conneau, Guillaume Lample, Marc'Aurelio Ranzato, Ludovic Denoyer, and Hervé Jégou. 2017. Word Translation without Parallel Data. *arXiv preprint arXiv:1710.04087* (2017). arXiv:1710.04087

Jacob Devlin, Ming-Wei Chang, Kenton Lee, and Kristina Toutanova. 2019. BERT: Pre-Training of Deep Bidirectional Transformers for Language Understanding. *arXiv:1810.04805 [cs]* (May 2019). arXiv:1810.04805 [cs]

Chris Emmery, Ben Verhoeven, Guy De Pauw, Gilles Jacobs, Cynthia Van Hee, Els Lefever, Bart Desmet,

Véronique Hoste, and Walter Daelemans. 2019. Current Limitations in Cyberbullying Detection: On Evaluation Criteria, Reproducibility, and Data Scarcity. *arXiv:1910.11922 [cs]* (Oct. 2019). arXiv:1910.11922 [cs]

Tom Fawcett. 2006. An Introduction to ROC Analysis. *Pattern recognition letters* 27, 8 (2006), 861–874.

Spiros V. Georgakopoulos, Sotiris K. Tasoulis, Aristidis G. Vrahatis, and Vassilis P. Plagianakos. 2018. Convolutional Neural Networks for Toxic Comment Classification. In *Proceedings of the 10th Hellenic Conference on Artificial Intelligence*. 1–6.

Sepp Hochreiter and Jürgen Schmidhuber. 1997. Long Short-Term Memory. *Neural Computation* 9, 8 (1997), 1735–1780. https://doi.org/10.1162/neco.1997.9.8.1735

Guillaume Lample, Alexis Conneau, Ludovic Denoyer, and Marc'Aurelio Ranzato. 2017. Unsupervised Machine Translation Using Monolingual Corpora Only. *arXiv preprint arXiv:1711.00043* (2017). arXiv:1711.00043

Jakub Nowak, Ahmet Taspinar, and Rafał Scherer. 2017. LSTM Recurrent Neural Networks for Short Text and Sentiment Classification. In *Artificial Intelligence and Soft Computing (Lecture Notes in Computer Science)*, Leszek Rutkowski, Marcin Korytkowski, Rafał Scherer, Ryszard Tadeusiewicz, Lotfi A. Zadeh, and Jacek M. Zurada (Eds.). Springer International Publishing, Cham, 553–562. https://doi.org/10.1007/978-3-319-59060-8_50

Endang Wahyu Pamungkas and Viviana Patti. 2019. Cross-Domain and Cross-Lingual Abusive Language Detection: A Hybrid Approach with Deep Learning and a Multilingual Lexicon. In *Proceedings of the 57th Annual Meeting of the Association for Computational Linguistics: Student Research Workshop*. Association for Computational Linguistics, Florence, Italy, 363–370. https://doi.org/10.18653/v1/P19-2051

Kartikey Pant and Tanvi Dadu. 2020. Cross-Lingual Inductive Transfer to Detect Offensive Language. *arXiv:2007.03771 [cs]* (July 2020). arXiv:2007.03771 [cs]

Zeinab Khatoun Pourtaheri and Seyed Hamid Zahiri. 2016. Ensemble Classifiers with Improved Overfitting. In *2016 1st Conference on Swarm Intelligence and Evolutionary Computation (CSIEC)*. 93–97. https://doi.org/10.1109/CSIEC.2016.7482130

Lukas Stappen, Fabian Brunn, and Björn Schuller. 2020. Cross-Lingual Zero- and Few-Shot Hate Speech Detection Utilising Frozen Transformer Language Models and AXEL. *arXiv:2004.13850 [cs, stat]* (April 2020). arXiv:2004.13850 [cs, stat]

Cynthia Van Hee, Els Lefever, Ben Verhoeven, Julie Mennes, Bart Desmet, Guy De Pauw, Walter Daelemans, and Véronique Hoste. 2015a. *Automatic Detection and Prevention of Cyberbullying*.

Cynthia Van Hee, Els Lefever, Ben Verhoeven, Julie Mennes, Bart Desmet, Guy De Pauw, Walter Daelemans, and Veronique Hoste. 2015b. Detection and Fine-Grained Classification of Cyberbullying Events. In *Proceedings of the International Conference Recent Advances in Natural Language Processing*. INCOMA Ltd. Shoumen, BULGARIA, Hissar, Bulgaria, 672–680.

Ashish Vaswani, Noam Shazeer, Niki Parmar, Jakob Uszkoreit, Llion Jones, Aidan N. Gomez, Lukasz Kaiser, and Illia Polosukhin. 2017. Attention Is All You Need. *arXiv:1706.03762 [cs]* (Dec. 2017). arXiv:1706.03762 [cs]

Ellery Wulczyn, Nithum Thain, and Lucas Dixon. 2017a. Ex Machina: Personal Attacks Seen at Scale. *arXiv:1610.08914 [cs]* (Feb. 2017). arXiv:1610.08914 [cs]

Ellery Wulczyn, Nithum Thain, and Lucas Dixon. 2017b. Ex Machina: Personal Attacks Seen at Scale. In *Proceedings of the 26th International Conference on World Wide Web*. 1391–1399.

Ellery Wulczyn, Nithum Thain, and Lucas Dixon. 2017c. Wikipedia Talk Labels: Personal Attacks. https://doi.org/10.6084/M9.FIGSHARE.4054689

S. Yadav and S. Shukla. 2016. Analysis of K-Fold Cross-Validation over Hold-Out Validation on Colossal Datasets for Quality Classification. In *2016 IEEE 6th International Conference on Advanced Computing (IACC)*. 78–83. https://doi.org/10.1109/IACC.2016.25

Zhuosheng Zhang, Yuwei Wu, Hai Zhao, Zuchao Li, Shuailiang Zhang, Xi Zhou, and Xiang Zhou. 2020. Semantics-Aware BERT for Language Understanding. *arXiv:1909.02209 [cs]* (Feb. 2020). arXiv:1909.02209 [cs]

Association for Computational Linguistics
209 N. Eighth Street
Stroudsburg, Pennsylvania 18360

ISBN 978-1-7138-4098-5

CURRAN ASSOCIATES INC.
proceedings.com